EMMA'S CHILD

A Play By

Kristine Thatcher

EMMA'S CHILD had its premiere performance at the Black Swan Theatre of the Oregon Shakespeare Festival, Ashland, Oregon, on April 1, 1995. It was directed by Cynthia White, with scenic design by Curt Enderle, costume design by Alvin Perry, and lighting design by Robert Peterson. The Music Director was Todd Barton. The cast and crew were as follows:

Jean Farrell	**LINDA EMOND**
Henry Farrell	**DAN KREMER**
Tess McGarrett	**DEBRA WICKS**
Franny Stornant	**KIRSTEN GIROUX**
Emma Miller	**CHRISTINE WILLIAMS**
Laurence	**RAY PORTER**
Mary Jo	**CINDY BASCO**
Vivien Rademacher	**JUDITH SANFORD**
Dr. Sarah Arbaugh	**DEBRA WICKS**
Sam Stornant	**MARK MURPHEY**
Michelle	**CHRISTINE WILLIAMS**

The Stage Manager was Katherine Gosnell, Assistant Stage Manager was Paula Donnelley, and the Properties Artisan was Paul James Martin.

ACT I

SCENE 1

[October, 1990. Place: A suggestion of the comfortable, but modest, home of Jean and Henry Farrell. There are bay windows, beyond which are shade trees in full autumn colors. A calico cat sleeps in a patch of sunlight. There are vases filled with the treasures of a backyard garden: roses, mums, dahlias, cosmos, catchlily, asters, and lime green grape vines. It is moments before Jean and Henry are to face an important interview. They are coming unglued. They burst into the room. Jean carries a tall vase filled with flowers.]

HENRY: I think it's better if you don't!

JEAN: Well, what am I gonna say, then?

HENRY: Tell them she died of natural causes.

JEAN: But, she didn't! Henry, don't move that vase. I just put it there.

HENRY: Jean, we'll be sitting around this coffee table. We won't be to able to see her.

JEAN: *[He's right.]* Dammit!

HENRY: I know you spent a lot of time on this stuff, but come on, I want a little eye contact with this woman. Besides, we're supposed to be presenting the every-day picture of how things work around here. We never have this many flowers. She's going to wonder where we're keeping the deceased.

JEAN: Well, thanks a lot!

1

HENRY: Just calm down, will you?

JEAN: <u>You</u> calm down.

HENRY: Can I move the vase?

JEAN: Move it!

HENRY: Where were we?

JEAN: What natural causes?

HENRY: Just say old age.

JEAN: She was sixty-three. She didn't go peacefully in her sleep.

HENRY: Can't you fudge it a little?

JEAN: Are you going to "fudge" when they ask about <u>your</u> health?

HENRY: All they have to do, Jean, is dig up a few medical records. I've been cancer-free for five years. What's the big deal?

JEAN: Then don't ask me to mess with my mother's liver!

HENRY: Oh, come on, it's not the same thing.

JEAN: My mother won't be raising this child! You will! You are not actually going to wear that sweater, are you?

HENRY: What's wrong with it?

JEAN: It's too small! What about the powder blue I gave you for Christmas?

HENRY: It won't go with these pants.

JEAN: Yes, it will!

HENRY: No, it won't! These pants are green!

JEAN: They're dark blue, Henry.

HENRY: No, they're not!

JEAN: Which of the two of us is color-blind!

HENRY: The powder blue itches. It makes my neck sweat.

JEAN: Go away! What did you want to ask me? You came in
here to ask me something?

HENRY: Where's the scouring powder?

JEAN: Don't tell me!

HENRY: Well, if you'd stop bitching for two minutes --

JEAN: Jesus. Jesus God.

HENRY: It's just the sink and the toilet! The floor is done!

JEAN: Give me one.

HENRY: No! Absolutely not!

JEAN: I may have to kill you, then.

HENRY: Jean, you have been smoke-free for eleven days.
When the caseworker asks whether we smoke, how would you
like to answer?

JEAN: Do you still have them?

HENRY: No.

JEAN: You destroyed them!

HENRY: Five minutes after you surrendered them!

JEAN: I'm going down to the corner. I'll be back in no time.

HENRY: The hell you are! This person is due here any minute.

JEAN: Then what about the sink and the toilet!

HENRY: And how you can talk about cigarettes, when we've just had a conversation about my cancer is beyond me! It's unconscionable!

JEAN: I've kept my smoke away from you. What I do in the backyard does not harm you. It is not your business!

HENRY: When you knowingly tamper with the well-being of my wife, it does harm me! It is my business! You have quit, Jean. It's been eleven days. Just stay quit!

JEAN: I want a divorce.

HENRY: You can have a divorce. What you can't have is a cigarette.
[The door-bell rings. They take a covert moment as everything changes.]
Come on, Jean.

JEAN: I can't make up a story, Hal.

HENRY: Neither can I.

4

JEAN: Fine.

HENRY: Do you really want a cigarette? I could --

JEAN: No. I'm just talking.

HENRY: Good.

JEAN: Maybe later.

HENRY: Here we go, then. Should I change?

JEAN: What?

HENRY: If these pants are blue --

JEAN: They <u>are</u> blue, but never mind. You look great. Open the door.

HENRY: You're ready?

JEAN: Yes.

[Cross-fade to Emma]

HENRY AND EMMA: Are you sure?

JEAN: *[Focused on Henry, but addressing Emma]* I'm sure.

[Henry exits.]

SCENE 2

[June, 1991. Place: The Newborn Special Care Unit at Christ Hospital. Center stage is Robin's home, an isolette with solid sides, so he is in no danger of rolling out. These also hide him from

audience view. He lies at the waist level of an adult. Attached to the up stage side of the isolette is a pole about six feet tall, and from that pole spreading out over the isolette is a roof or hood, containing temperature and light controls. We never see this child. He is always covered or swaddled. Nearby is a small machine that monitors his vital signs. Stage right center is a comfortable rocking chair and a small table.]

EMMA: Henry couldn't make it?

JEAN: *[Turning to Emma]* I beg your pardon?

EMMA: Henry flaked out?

JEAN: He had to work.

EMMA: Right.

JEAN: He really did have to work, Emma.

EMMA: Are you ready?

JEAN: Yes.

EMMA: I don't want to force you.

JEAN: I just didn't think they'd let me see him, that's all.

EMMA: He's right here.
          [They approach and peer into the crib]
Hi, Blue Bear. There's the guy! Hi, Blueberry.

JEAN *[Drinking him in, which takes a neutral second]*: Hello, Robin.

EMMA: Whatchoo doin' today? Whatchoo doin'? *[To Jean:]* Do you see?

JEAN: Yes.

EMMA: You see?

JEAN: Oh, yes.

EMMA: Whatchoo doin', Blue Bear? How's my Blue Bear?

JEAN: Hi, Baby.

EMMA: I think old Larry must have wondered what happened to me.

JEAN: Larry?

EMMA: Laurence. The nurse. He may be a fruit loop, I don't know.

JEAN: Oh.

EMMA: I think he's pissed because I haven't been here. He gives me these looks.

JEAN: Oh, no. I'm sure he...

EMMA: It's hard to get away. It's over an hour from Joliet. And I got a summer job with the Park District now.

JEAN: I'm sure he understands.

EMMA: I don't have my own car.

JEAN: He understands.

EMMA: I wish I could, but I can't. Plus, Michael's walkin' and climbin'. He's a tornado. Yesterday he pulled a chest of drawers down on himself. I like to be with him when he's awake, because

7

he could just croak himself any minute now. He don't understand about gravity yet. My dad keeps sayin', "He's got a date with Mr. Gravity! " So I kinda wanna be around when the introductions are made, you know?

JEAN *[intensely focused on the baby]*: Is he okay? Does he --?

EMMA: He does that when he's sleepy. It's spooky, but he don't really have a grip on his eyes.

JEAN: Oh. So he's --

EMMA: It's just a sign he's gettin' sleepy. *[To Jean:]* They already told me he's not gonna make it.

JEAN: Who told you?

EMMA: Doctor Arbaugh. Somethin' about the stuff in his head. I said it was okay not to revive him if something should happen. Do you think that was wise? I don't know.

JEAN: I don't know either, Emma. They've told me a little, but I still have so many questions.

EMMA: You know, they didn't tell me for four days after he was born. They kept me knocked out. And every time I woke up, I'd ask them where you were, and if he was healthy, and if you liked each other. And they always said, "Oh, yes. Yes."

JEAN: I had to cut through a lot of red tape to get here.

EMMA: Somewhere under all those drugs, I knew something was going on.

JEAN: Does the doctor come by often?

EMMA: I don't know. I talked to her on the phone. This is only the third time I've been here.

JEAN: Oh.

EMMA: I <u>want</u> to come. I had to borrow my dad's truck to meet you here today.

JEAN: It's okay, Emma.

EMMA: He looks kind of pathetic, don't he? He don't have no clothes or nothin'. I brought him some of Michael's baby stuff, but I just didn't keep that much. They're all dirty now, and -- it don't look like anybody around here does personal laundry. His diapers are always clean when I come. Still, he's got a pretty bad rash. *[Hopefully:]* Do you want to hold him?

JEAN: No, not yet.
    [One of Robin's machines starts to beep.]
What's that sound?

EMMA: It's one of his monitors. I've seen 'em flip it off here.
    [She swats at a switch and the sound stops.]
There.

JEAN: Shouldn't we call someone?

EMMA: If there's a real problem, it makes another sound.

JEAN: What does it monitor?

EMMA: Got me. I can't figure it out. *[To the baby]* But, you're okay, aren't ya, Baby Bear. He looks like his father. Funny how he turned out. Jamie is so smart. He was always doin' the kind of math that didn't even look like numbers, know what I mean? Just, all these crazy squiggles on the page? And it's not just math; he was always after me about how bad I spoke. I probably should have paid more attention to it when I had the chance. And he has

9

these blue-ice eyes, that smack out of his face. He is <u>good</u>
<u>lookin'</u>, *[To the baby:]* just like you, Blue Bear.
[To Jean]
I never thought I'd see Jamie again. Somebody from the bar said
they saw him out with my mother a while ago. But, I don't
believe that.

JEAN: Your mother?

EMMA: On a date.

JEAN: I'm sorry?

EMMA: The guy who told me is full of crap. I mean, <u>she</u>
probably would, she <u>would</u>. But she's the last thing in the world
Jamie would go for. She's thirty-five years old! Just to give you
an idea? No offense.

JEAN: None taken.

EMMA: 'Member that cold snap about a week ago? I ran into him
about that time. Just walkin' the street, his arms full of books.
He invited me for a beer. It was like some weird dream. We sat
there, at the same table. The music was the same, the people was
the same. I could see that look in his eyes, and hear that thing in
his voice. The only difference -- I was in stitches. No joke! I
mean, I really <u>was</u> -- I was in --

JEAN: They hadn't removed your stitches.

EMMA: I still <u>had</u> 'em. So, at the bar, that night, I let him come
on in the same old way. I didn't hear nothin' new, but, I was
<u>seein'</u> for the first time since he dumped me. He was <u>some</u> frat
rat, and I was just a local nuthin'. It was cold, and I was wearin'
cutoffs, and, I don't know, he pissed me off. So, for no reason,
alls a sudden, I open my bag and take out a xerox of Robin's
footprints, and I put the paper down -- bang - right there on the

table. Jamie looked at it, and he stopped breathing, just like that. I told him I wasn't comin after nuthin'. And I told him what a poor condition his little boy was in. He listened, and he listened, and when he finally talked, he asked a lot of questions. I told him about you guys. I told him about the monitors, and the tubes, and the sirens. So, he starts snifflin' and cryin'. Give me a break! And he goes, "Can I come up with you some time and see little Robin?" And I'm like, you're kiddin' me! So, I say to him, I go, "No way. No way in this wide world will you ever lay eyes on that boy." I know he's the father, and he's probably got rights, but I don't want him near this child. And I don't think he'll sue me or nuthin'. But, even if he does, I won't have him around. Okay?

JEAN: It's fine by me.

EMMA *[Looking down at Robin]*: Hey, Fellah.
　　　　[She reaches for a jar under the isolette]
This is the stuff they put on his rash.

JEAN: That's good.
　　　　[There is a silence.]

EMMA: You know how the agency shows those family album deals?

JEAN: Yah.

EMMA: I had it narrowed down to you and one other couple. They had a seven-year-old boy, and I thought it might be nice for the baby to have an older brother. But that night I had a dream, and I saw you. My dad thinks dreams are God talkin' in your ear, tellin' you what to do. I like that. Course, at the time I had this dream, I thought Robin was gonna be healthy. I thought he was gonna be some great gift.
　　　　[Beat]
He needs clothes.

11

JEAN *[Silence]*: I have clothes.

EMMA: I thought you might.

JEAN: They were meant for him.

EMMA: He needs clean things.

JEAN: I have things. I'll bring them.

EMMA: He needs cuddlin' or somethin'. You want to hold him?

JEAN: Not yet.

EMMA: I'm supposed to have the truck back by four. My dad's gotta go to work.

JEAN: You're leaving?

EMMA: I'd better get goin'.

JEAN: Oh.

EMMA: He's no trouble. My dad's gotta work, and ...

JEAN: And Michael has that date with Mr. Gravity.

EMMA: Right. I kinda gotta be there for that.

JEAN: Sure.

EMMA *[She smiles hard at the baby]:* Blueberry! Baby Bear! Don't be shy now. *[She turns to go.]*

JEAN: Emma!

EMMA Yeah?

JEAN *[Changing her mind]*: Keep in touch.
[Emma gives a cynical wave, and goes. Jean looks down at the child.]
So, Robin. Well, now.
[A beat]
I hear you've got some kind of crazy diaper rash.
[Calculating how one goes about it, she picks up a towel and slings it over her shoulder. She awkwardly locates and gathers the things she'll need for the change, then turns her attention to Robin.]
Now, how do we, uh -- ? Oh, these -- right, these tabby things -- We'll give it the old college -
[She opens the diaper, and peers at its contents.]
Whoa. Whoa!
[She looks around for a nurse, then back to Robin. She looks around again.]
Nurse?

[Cross-fade begins. Tess enters the Farrell living room.]

Could somebody help me?

SCENE 3

[Tess and Henry have just finished a tour of the house. They are four hours into the homestudy. In the shadows around the isolette, Jean tackles the diaper change on her own under the ensuing dialogue.]

TESS: That about wraps up the tour of the house. Oh, yes, one more thing. Do you have any smoke detectors or fire alarms?

13

HENRY *[who is coming in just behind her]*: What? Uh, no.
No. Nothing like that.

TESS: No?

HENRY: No. We don't believe in them.

TESS: May I ask why not?

HENRY: We don't think they're necessary.

TESS: They save lives, Mr. Farrell.

HENRY: I'm sorry?

TESS: They save lives.

HENRY *[A beat, while he enters the Twilight Zone.]*: Frankly, I
won't have one in my home.

TESS: The state requires them.

HENRY: You're kidding. No, they don't.

TESS: *[Another beat, while she joins him there.]*: Why -- why
are you so opposed to them? Is it the cost?

HENRY: It's the principle.

TESS *[Beat]*: Because they are very inexpensive. You can pick
them up at any discount store.

HENRY: I realize that.

TESS: If you want to be licensed to adopt, you'll have to get
one.

HENRY *[Beat]*: Are we by any chance having the same conversation?

TESS: Boy, you know, that's what I'm wondering.

HENRY: I'm talking about guns. What are you talking about?

TESS: Guns!

HENRY: Right. Fire arms. Didn't you say fire arms?

TESS: I said smoke detectors or fire alarms.

HENRY: Oh!

TESS: Oh!

HENRY: Fire <u>alarms!</u>

TESS: Yes.

HENRY: I thought you were going to make me get a pistol or something. It made no sense.

TESS: And it was going so well up until then.

HENRY: It was, wasn't it?
> *[They chuckle.]*

TESS: I guess I don't need to ask you about guns now, do I?

HENRY *[Another polite chuckle]*: I'm sorry. I get hard of hearing when I'm nervous.

TESS: You're not nervous, are you?

HENRY: Oh, we've been -- we have been a little nuts.

15

JEAN [*Entering with the towel, wiping her hands*]: How was the tour. Did we pass?

HENRY [*Rising*]: Why don't you take over.

TESS: Henry thinks he blew it.

JEAN: He does, does he?..... [*A trifle dangerously*] Did he?

TESS: No, he's doing fine.

JEAN: You told her about my politics, eh?

HENRY: No, I told her about our sex life.

JEAN: What's that?

HENRY: A joke, honey.

TESS: He told me about your smoke detectors.

JEAN: Are the batteries dead?

HENRY: No. Never mind.

TESS: Lunch was excellent. We should have helped you with the dishes.

JEAN: No trouble at all.

TESS: I have one more question, and then I'll be out of your way. How are you holding up?

JEAN: Fine.

HENRY: Great.

TESS: This one is sometimes the most difficult. I should probably start with it, but --

JEAN: Go ahead. Fire away.

TESS: What kind of baby do you want?

JEAN: What do we want?

TESS: What kind?

JEAN *[Laughs]*: Any old kind.

TESS: I mean, what are your limits? I think you made it clear earlier you want an infant, no older than eight months?

JEAN: Does that limit us? It's just that we don't want to miss out on parenting an infant. Chances are, this will be our only child.

TESS: It's fine. It's your choice. What else? Would you be willing to take a child of color?

JEAN: Yes.

HENRY: I don't know.

TESS: *[focusing on Henry, but without judgment]*: Mixed-race? Caucasian-Hispanic?

JEAN: Yes.

HENRY: Uh- yeah, I guess.

TESS: Asian-Caucasian?

HENRY: Mm-hmm.

JEAN: Yes.

TESS: Caucasian-black?

JEAN: Yes.

HENRY: Um -- if you want to know what my ideal child would be like -- it would be -- uh, caucasian.

TESS *[ignoring Jean now]*: That's fine. Boy, girl?

JEAN: Either.

HENRY: A girl is my preference, though, I'd take a boy, too.

TESS: Would you be willing to take a child with mental or emotional disabilities?

HENRY: No.

JEAN: I don't know. Our ideal child would be healthy.

TESS: What about physical disabilities?

JEAN: I can't say no, just like that. I very well might.

HENRY: I would consider taking a child with correctable or minor physical problems.

TESS: Cleft palate, club foot, along those lines?

HENRY: Yes. But nothing major. I'm not cut out to be - I know what I can do.

TESS *[Reassuring him]*: That's fine, Henry. We want the clearest possible picture of the child you want. Where Jean is concerned, a child of color or mixed heritage would be fine.

She would also be willing to consider a child with disabilities. Where you are concerned, a healthy, caucasian infant girl would do the trick, though you would accept a boy. Is this right?

HENRY: It's rigid, probably.

TESS: It's specific. We want to find these children the parents they were meant to have. It may mean you'll wait a bit longer.

HENRY: That's fine. We've waited a long time already. We're good at waiting.

TESS: Your patience will pay. Listen, I should get going. I have another homestudy tonight at six, and I need to get to my own home first. I hate to eat and run.

JEAN: It's over? That was it?

TESS: It wasn't so bad, was it?

JEAN: No.

HENRY: It was fine.

TESS *[Gathering her things]*: You should be hearing from the agency in a couple of weeks.

JEAN: That's -- two weeks.

TESS: Fourteen days.

HENRY: Thank you.

TESS: No problem. My pleasure, actually. What did you do with my coat, Henry?

HENRY: I'll get it.

TESS: Nice meeting you, Jean. The flowers are great.

JEAN: Yes.

TESS: Take it easy.

JEAN: I will. I do.

TESS: Bye, now.

JEAN: Bye.
  [After Tess is gone, and to no one in particular.]
Thank you.

[Black out]

ACT II

SCENE 1

[Time: June, 1991. Place: The Farrell living room. The shade trees through the window bear the green leaves of summer. A vase of peonies sits on the table. Franny stands in middle of the living room.]

FRANNY: Where did he go?

JEAN: No doubt he dumped the bags in your room, and made a bee-line for his office.

FRANNY: Novel?

JEAN: No, he's paying the bills today. He's doing a feature on the pros and cons of riverboat gambling for the Trib. Unfortunately, he's having a little trouble focusing. Thank you for coming, Fran.

FRANNY *[Removing her jacket]*: I wouldn't have missed the birth of this child for the world, are you kidding?

JEAN: My God, woman, how much weight have you lost?

FRANNY: Fifteen, maybe.

JEAN: I don't think I've ever seen you with your hair long.
                    [Or short, depending.]
Franny, you look fabulous. Are you in love, or what?

FRANNY: You know, I was trying to figure out on the plane how long you've waited for this baby. You stopped using birth control, when? Seventy-seven?

21

JEAN: Seventy-six. The bicentennial. July 4th, at Glenn Lake, remember?

FRANNY: Eric Tull got drunk on Sangria, recited the Gettysburg Address from memory, and vomited into the kitchen sink.

JEAN: We lit sparklers to commemorate the occasion.

FRANNY: That's fifteen years ago.

JEAN: A helluva long pregnancy.

FRANNY: I believe only the pterodactyl takes longer to reproduce itself.

JEAN: I believe you're right.

FRANNY: Are you stunned? You seem kind of --

JEAN: I still can't get over the fact that Emma chose us. It's a little like getting hit by an ice cream truck. Fairly shocking, but still, you're lying in a puddle of Haagen Das.

FRANNY: Might as well grab a spoon.

JEAN: Precisely.

FRANNY: Show me this birthing kit you've put together.

JEAN: I have an expert on the scene, at last. You're my salvation.

FRANNY: I don't know how expert I am. Every birth is different.

JEAN: It's the birth-partnering books, Franny. They're driving me insane! Why I ever agreed to coach her through labor, I will never know.

FRANNY: One thing at a time.

JEAN: Okay. The birthing kit:
[She grabs the tote bag and starts tossing things out of it.]
Hal made me these charts to keep track of the time between
contractions. Massage oil, unscented, in case she's feeling
nauseous.

FRANNY: Pay attention to the lower back.

JEAN: Right. A cold pack for chipped ice in case she wants to
suck. Bubble bath, a manicure kit, moisturizers, a deck of
cards.

FRANNY: Are you planning to be there a few days?

JEAN: I thought if the labor is long, we'd just have some fun.
[Franny hoots.]
Is this, like, too stupid?

FRANNY: Not at all. Keep going.

JEAN: My favorite blue ice skating socks. I read somewhere
their feet get cold.

FRANNY: Nice touch.

JEAN: Champagne, three glasses. A dozen roses -- that's Hal's
job, on the day.

FRANNY: Excellent.

JEAN: I want her to know how grateful we are. She couldn't be
doing more for us if she was donating a vital organ: her lungs.
Her heart.

FRANNY: Tell me about the books.

JEAN: They're making me nuts!

FRANNY So you said.

JEAN: The way they breathe is important. That's the main thing, right?

FRANNY: Just go.

JEAN: Okay. During the early stages of labor, when a contraction hits, I'm supposed to encourage her to take a deep, cleansing breath, followed by six to nine chest inhalation-exhalations. We conclude with another cleansing breath. During the accelerated phase, she takes a cleansing breath, and then I encourage her to pant as the wave rises.

FRANNY: Jean?

JEAN: What?

FRANNY: The way they breathe ain't diddly.

JEAN: What? No.

FRANNY: That's the trouble with book learning, okay? I've been there hundreds of times, and I'm telling you: the breathing stuff is basically bullshit.

JEAN: Then, I'm lost.

FRANNY: Breathing techniques are like that deck of cards in your bag. They distract you while this unbelievable thing is happening to your body. Breathing is important when a woman gets nervous, or scared. It's important when the baby's head is crowning, and they don't want him to come out too fast. So, they tell her to blow -- like she's blowing out a candle. Yes?

JEAN: Yes.

FRANNY: A good birth partner is someone who can keep a sense of humor, without being intrusive. She knows when to leave you alone if you want to shut down, and she can lead you with a clear, rational mind when yours is full of obscenities.

JEAN: Great. I've met this woman twice.

FRANNY: So what? Even if you screw up, what choice will Emma have? Let's face it, the child is a big thing, and it has to come out one way or another. I've seen birth partners hyperventilate and pass out on the floor. I've heard them crying for their own mothers. The woman who is giving birth still finds a way to get that baby out, no matter what kind of blithering idiot is holding her hand.

JEAN: The upshot is that any moron can be a birth partner, is that right?

FRANNY: I'm glad to see you're following me here. Just be sensitive to when she wants your touch and when she loathes it. The same thing goes for the sound of your voice.

JEAN: This is something you can describe for a million years, but a woman like me will never get it.

FRANNY: Sort out the little things for her. Deal with the demanding people around her when she can't. *[The phone rings.]* Feed her chipped ice. Shall I pick up?

JEAN: Maybe it's the hospital.
                    [She quickly repacks the bag.]

FRANNY: Hello? ... Relax. It's for me. Henry? ... No, I've got it ... Go back to work. It's not the hospital, it's for me... Yeah. Try to relax.
                    [She returns to the phone]
Hi, there. It was Hal... Very nice voice ... Yes, I made it... It wasn't too bad.

JEAN: Yo, Sam.
                    25

FRANNY: I don't think so. Not tonight.

JEAN: Tell him Henry got the cigars.

FRANNY: Tomorrow afternoon maybe... There's a lot going on around here ... I know.... No, I haven't .... I will, I will...

JEAN: Let me talk to him when you're done.

FRANNY: I have to go... Yes, I have the number.... I miss you, too.

JEAN: Let me talk to him.

FRANNY: Me, too... Me, too. Bye.
                              [She hangs up.]

JEAN *[surprised]*: Franny! I wanted to talk to him.

FRANNY: Jean --

JEAN *[After a second]*: That wasn't Sam, was it?

FRANNY No.

JEAN: Who was that?

FRANNY: It wasn't Sam.

JEAN: Who was it?

FRANNY: Scott.

JEAN *[Cautiously]*: Old friend?

FRANNY: New.

JEAN: Oh, my God.

FRANNY: I've wanted to tell you. I couldn't do it long distance.

[The phone rings again.]
I needed your face.
[Pause while they make certain it doesn't ring again. Henry has grabbed it.]

JEAN: Lives here in Chicago, does he?

FRANNY: No. He -- followed me here.

JEAN: He ... <u>followed</u> you?

FRANNY: This probably isn't the best time to talk about it.

JEAN: What about Sam?

FRANNY: I don't know, Jean. I'm going to take a month away, just to think things through. If I can't stay here, I'll go to my sister in Evanston.

JEAN: Won't it be rather difficult to think rationally with this Scott person following you around?

FRANNY: Jean, I want you to meet him. He's wonderful.

JEAN: Franny, Sam has been my friend for seventeen years.

FRANNY: I know.

JEAN *[Beat]*: I need an iced tea, or some soda. You want anything?

FRANNY: Wait, Jean.

JEAN: Just give me a minute, okay?

HENRY *[Headlong entrance]*: Jean, that was Tess on the phone.

27

JEAN: What are you saying? Do we go?

HENRY: Not yet. We're supposed to hang tight. Emma just went to the hospital. Her water broke. She's being examined. They don't want us to come yet.

JEAN: It's seventy miles to Silver Cross --

HENRY: Even so, they want us to stay right here for the moment. Tess'll call within the hour. There may be some problem, honey.

JEAN: What problem?

HENRY: Nothing serious. They may have to deliver by C-section, that's all Tess said.

JEAN: Why? What's the matter?

HENRY: Jean, she didn't say.

FRANNY: Maybe they can't get the baby to turn.

HENRY: Tess says we should still get ready. If they decide to let her deliver vaginally, they expect it will be a long labor. We'll have plenty of time to get there.

FRANNY: This is it, Jean!

JEAN: Right.

FRANNY: What do you want to do? What should we do?

HENRY: We're packed. We just need to kill some time until the phone rings again. Maybe get into comfortable clothing.

FRANNY: Sneakers.

HENRY: I need to find my cigars.

JEAN *[To Henry, demanding]*: Where's the hammer?

HENRY: The hammer?

JEAN: The hammer! The hammer! How many times do I have to say it? The hammer!

HENRY: Basement stairwell. On the hook. Same as always. Where are you going?

JEAN *[She grabs up the birthing kit bag.]*: I'll be back.
                              [Jean exits.]

HENRY: What is she doing?

                    [Cross-fade begins.]

SCENE 2

[July, 1991, the hospital. Jean crosses quickly and ties on her robe.]

JEAN *[At the isolette, beaming down at Robin]*: Don't look at me like that, I told you I'd be back.

FRANNY: My best guess is that she's going to go chip some ice.

                    [The cross-fade is complete.]

JEAN: What've we got today? *[She rummages in her bag.]* Look at this: a music box! It plays the theme from Zeferelli's <u>Romeo and Juliet</u>. My Grandparents gave it to me after a certain trip to Las Vegas that looms legendary in family lore. It had something to do with forgetting where they parked their Buick, and having to wire home for money. They lost their car, but they remembered to bring me this. I've been saving it all these years for my own child. I thought maybe you could -- well, here it is. It's an insistent little tune, but, it will give you a break from these crazy sirens. There is such a thing as music, Robin.

[She winds it up, opens the lid, and places it next to his ear.]
You like that?

[He does.]

And this is nothing. There is a corporation called Muzak that does a whole lot better than this. Okay, what else have we got?

[Into her bag again, she pulls out a stuffed doll.]
Ah, yes. Humpty Dumpty. This guy could be your brother, no kidding -- look at that noggin'. I'm gonna tuck him in with you, because, when I'm not around, I figure you can use a friend, right? So just -- you know, talk to him. Ask him stuff.

[Going right for the diaper, we hear the tabs.]
I gotta tell ya, kiddo, I hate this part.

[She peels it back.]
Whoa -- still pretty bad. Does it hurt? Does it sting?
[Looking up and around, but proceeding to change him rather awkwardly.]
Do these sirens get on your nerves, or what?

LAURENCE: Mrs. Farrell? You asked for me?

JEAN: Laurence. Have I taken you away from somebody?

LAURENCE: No, no. What can I do for you? You've got it on backwards.

JEAN: What?

LAURENCE: His diaper. Teddy bears in front.

JEAN: Oh. I'm new at this.

LAURENCE: It's okay.

JEAN: I have a bunch of questions.

LAURENCE: I'm not surprised.

JEAN: Good.

LAURENCE: Shoot.

JEAN: First, I would like to know where I am. Most of these babies are pretty small.

LAURENCE: Premies-R-Us, yes.

JEAN: This little one over here -- he -- she? -- will go home? I saw the mother here the other day; they'll go home together?

LAURENCE: That's right. That's baby Angela. She's a twin. Sister Letitia is down the way there.

JEAN: They'll go home?

LAURENCE: That's what we're hoping. Mom is in drug rehab.

JEAN: Oh, I see.

LAURENCE: Keep your fingers crossed.

[Robin's machine whines. Laurence flips the switch.]

JEAN: Why did it beep? What does it mean?

LAURENCE: Time to change his IV, that's all.
[He proceeds to do so during the course of their conversation.]
If there's a real emergency, you'll know it. More questions?

JEAN: Boy, that makes me nuts, that sound.

LAURENCE: You get used to it.

31

JEAN: So, is there anybody else here like Robin? Same problems? Similar problems?

LAURENCE: No, 'fraid not.

JEAN *[Disappointed]*: Oh. *[To the baby:]* You're a trail-blazer, Kid.

LAURENCE: Not exactly. We've seen little guys like Robin in the past. What else?

JEAN: The diaper rash, what is that? I mean, come on -- can't we-- ?

LAURENCE: He gets away from us sometimes. Emergencies crop up. We're understaffed. It means that every once in a while he has to lie in it. We do our best, Mrs. Farrell.

JEAN: I'm sure you do, but he--

LAURENCE: Are you going to be around during visitor's hours?

JEAN: Yes.

LAURENCE: You've located the diapers and ointment. Very good. When you help us, you're helping him.

JEAN: I see. All right. Now, it's about this nose-tube.

LAURENCE: Yes?

JEAN: He keeps trying to pull it out. It must be very irritating.

LAURENCE: That's a safe assumption.

JEAN: He wants it gone. He wants to be treated like a person. He wants to try the bottle again.

LAURENCE: He told you this?

JEAN: Yeah, he wants to belly up to the bar like the midgets over there.

LAURENCE: He won't suck. He's deficient in the sucking arena.

JEAN *[To the baby]*: Are you gonna lie there and listen to this?
[To Laurence:]
He sucks the tip of my little finger.

LAURENCE: *[Mildly appalled]*: You put your finger in his mouth?

JEAN: I cut my nails; there's no polish. It's clean.

LAURENCE: And he sucks it?

JEAN: Like a leech.

LAURENCE: Mrs. Farrell --

JEAN: Jean.

LAURENCE: Jean, you may be getting your hopes up here for no --

JEAN: If he doesn't eat, we put the hose right back.

LAURENCE *[Beat]*: Sounds good to me.

JEAN: Simple.

LAURENCE: I'll speak to the doctor.

JEAN: So, tell me about the machinery.

LAURENCE: We're monitoring his lungs and his heart, among other things. Blood pressure pops up here. This little gizmo tells me what the temperature of his environment is.
[He pats the machine.]

JEAN: Should I be careful about exciting him? His heart and his lungs are weak?

LAURENCE: Actually, no, this is all standard procedure for a newborn like Robin.

JEAN: Then, I can give him a little exercise?

LAURENCE: I don't know what you have in mind, but, if we're talking baby aerobics, he's probably game.

JEAN: How often does his doctor come along? Dr. Arbaugh? I would like to catch her.

LAURENCE: Once a day, about seven in the morning.

JEAN: That's before visiting hours.

LAURENCE: Right, but I could set up an appointment for you later in the day, if you want.

JEAN: I do want.

LAURENCE: Stop by the desk on your way out, and we'll give her office a call.

JEAN: Great.

LAURENCE: I like his outfit.

JEAN: Well, we're trying to create some excitement around here.

LAURENCE: The socks do it. I'm a sucker for argyle. What

else?

JEAN: Can one -- maybe --?

LAURENCE: What?

JEAN: Pick him up? Hold him? I see that rocking thing there.
Would he like to change his environment, or do you think that
would be -- ? That's probably a bit much.

LAURENCE: Oh, that would be fabulous.

JEAN: Well, yeah, but -- we're talking a -- water balloon here!

LAURENCE: Sit down.
[Indicating the pillow lying on the seat of the chair.]
Take that pillow for your arm, and make yourself comfy.

JEAN: Really?

LAURENCE: Have a seat.

JEAN: He won't mind?

LAURENCE: I'd say, it will be the equivalent of -- oh -- pick
any ride at Disneyland.

JEAN: Okay.

LAURENCE: It's better if two of us do it. I'm going to get
Mary Jo, I'll be right back.
[He exits.]

JEAN: Okay. *[She gets up and leans into the isolette]*
We're going to try something here, Baby. "Pirates of the
Carribean" coming up. If you don't panic, I won't. If at any
point you hate this, however, just call out, all right? Boom!
Back in the old isolette, okay?

35

[Looking at his face,]
What a name for a bed. Isolette.
[Rising to a certain challenge]
You needn't look so all alone, Gummy. We have a certain
amount of experience on which to draw. You're not the first. I
met someone like you once before. It was during a field trip
with Mr. Garchow -- *[Pronounced "Gar-shaw"]* eighth-grade
social studies -- to the Coldwater State Hospital.
*[As she speaks she takes brand-new clothing out of a bag, and
puts it away. She rips price tags from a few items. Then she
takes Robin's dirty laundry from under the isolette, and stuffs it
in her bag.]*
My mother used to say I came back from that trip another
person. She felt I was diminished in some way. Little did she
know. I remember that it was the kind of pristine winter day
we only used to get when I was a kid. We bumped along in a
big yellow bus. There was a rowdy cheerfulness, because we
were free, my classmates and I, from spending another day in
the slammer. When we arrived, we went to an orientation with
some droner in a white suit. There was a tour of the offices,
the cafeteria, the laundry facilities. It seems to me we plunged
right in after that, we innocents abroad, and walked among the
less fortunate. We saw the mongoloid babies with their high-
pitched cries; young women, shredding their hair and skins; and
old men, deserted, wailing, clad only in diapers. There was a
place, fittingly called "the rec room", and as our line snaked
through, we met "the very wanderers of the dark". I found I
couldn't keep my limbs still, or catch a decent breath. I
couldn't hold one thought in my head. To think she lived with
those sounds, day and night. By the time we bottle-necked, just
outside her room, I was almost hallucinating. I kept my eyes
focused on the shafts of sunlight coming through the hall
window. It was Lutheran-Jesus-type light. You know, those
pictures? You'd swear the Man was coming out of a hole in the
clouds; swear he was going to just walk down a golden path of
light and cue up at the end of the line. I was behind Bev
Tucker, class vice-president and redhead extraordinaire. She
might as well have been reporting the crash of the Hindenberg

36

to millions of Americans: *[Without sarcasm]* "My God, you won't believe this. Wisps of hair, on a <u>horse's</u> head. Her eyes must be <u>five</u> inches apart. They have to turn her twice a day. Pass it on. Her name is Debbie, she's nine years old, pass it on." *[Beat]* Debbie lay in a room with doors at either end, so we could conveniently file in one, and out the other. The rays streamed into her quiet crib as I came near. Out of the corner of my eye, I saw her awesome shape. *[She gently touches the child.]* Not unlike yours, my boy. I also saw she kept her eyes cast down on the bed sheets as Bev went by. I decided I wouldn't look, either, as I took my turn before her. And, then, we both surprised ourselves: she looked up, and I looked down. In that one moment, I saw her daring! I saw her humor, and her intelligence. I saw her vigilance; her never-ending patience; her sweet, forgiving soul. Never before, and certainly not since, have I seen a face so loving and open. I've often wondered: in that instant, when we looked at one another, what did <u>she</u> see? I hope she saw someone who took what she had to give, but I don't know if she did. I don't think she did.
>   *[She looks down at Robin]*
Hell, she must have been quite the philosopher by then. It probably didn't matter. I wonder if she's still alive..... I wonder if she sees you. If she sees you, I wonder what she would say to you.

HENRY *[Entering in the dark with a large tray that he deposits on the coffee table]*: Lemon chicken, for Chrissake.

JEAN: What wonderful thing would she say?

HENRY: Pot stickers.

JEAN: I want to say it.

>   *[Cross-fade to Henry. Jean is in the dark.]*

Scene 3

[It is mid-June, three days after Robin's birth, 11:30 at night in the Farrell living room. Exhausted, but engaged, Henry hunches over white cartons on the coffee table. Jean returns with a fresh glass of wine.]

HENRY: Pot stickers are your favorite. Try the watermelon. It's from the Oak Street Market.

JEAN: Since when? I was there yesterday.

HENRY: Six o'clock this morning. That clerk you like --

JEAN: Isabel.

HENRY: She told me herself the first shipment of the season came in this morning at six.

JEAN: It looks good.

HENRY: You've been saying that since nine o'clock.

JEAN: It's looked good since nine o'clock.

HENRY: Then put down the wine glass, and eat some of it.

JEAN: Sing your part by yourself one more time, and then I'll add the harmony. "O, Come All Ye Faithful": here we go.

HENRY: Why do you torture me?

JEAN: You almost have it.

HENRY: Please. I have a five-note range.

JEAN: You exaggerate.

HENRY: Then why, in God's name, do you want to hear me sing Christmas carols?

JEAN: I love it when you sing.

HENRY: In the middle of June, no less.

JEAN: I can conjure you at age thirteen when you sing. It's just possible I married you for your singing voice. Stop looking at me like you're the last sane person on earth.

HENRY: You don't think I am?

JEAN: That's beside the point. Sanity shouldn't flaunt itself. Come on. OH, COME ALL YE FAITHFUL" ("All" and "ful" -- same note.)

HENRY: Shh!

JEAN: What?

HENRY: Franny's sleeping.

JEAN: And where was she all afternoon and evening, that's what I want to know! Why does she feel she has to go sneaking around with that Todd-person?

HENRY: When you can handle the information without referring to the man as "that Todd-person", I'm sure she'll tell you.

JEAN: Okay. I'm sorry. Todd. Simply Todd. I'm sure Todd is a fine, decent --

HENRY: His name is Scott, Jean.

JEAN: *[Beat]* Let's try "Joy to the World" again. You've got that pretty good. Just remember: *[She sings the harmony part]* "JOY TO THE WORLD THE LORD (go down on "LORD") IS

39

COME"

HENRY: No.

JEAN: Do it! Just let loose. Set yourself free.

HENRY: Not until you give equal time to Hanukkah. Let's do "Dianu".

JEAN: Far be it from me to slam your heritage, but "Dianu" is a bore, Henry.

HENRY: It is not a bore!
[He sings it. She joins him. They stop and look at each other.]
Okay, it's a bore.
[One last attempt]
You got a nice piece of fruit there. Fresh off the vine, I swear. Any nutrition is better than no --

JEAN: "Nice piece of fruit"? I "got a nice piece of fruit"?

HENRY: I sound like my mother, is that what you're saying?

JEAN: I didn't say it.

HENRY: But that's what you're thinking.

JEAN: I'm glad you asked. You know what I'm thinking, honey?

HENRY: Oh, Christ.

JEAN: No, go ahead. You know what I'm <u>really</u> thinking?

HENRY: Okay, let me see. You are silently musing on Moliere's astute observation that "It's good food and not fine words" that keeps us alive.

JEAN: Nice try, but no.

HENRY *[Beat]*: Then you agree with Fielding that there is at least one fool in every married couple.

JEAN *[Beat]*: I don't want to hurt your feelings, Hal, but I really wasn't thinking about you.

HENRY: At this particular point in time.

JEAN: Not at this time, no.

HENRY: Then -- what first occurred to me, and I don't know why the hell I didn't say it right off --

JEAN: Go ahead.

HENRY: You're about to suggest that if we save the seeds from this rotting watermelon, we can make a fortune manufacturing maracas.

JEAN *[Beat]*: You amaze me.

HENRY: I got it right?

JEAN: No.

HENRY: If that isn't it, then, gosh, I give up. I really can't imagine what you're thinking. I'm afraid you're going to have to <u>tell</u> me.

JEAN: I'm thinking I'd like to go up to the hospital to see Emma.

HENRY *[Genuinely surprised]*: Oh.

JEAN: What do <u>you</u> think?

41

HENRY: Don't they usually let the mother go home after two days or so?

JEAN: Not with a C-section. Tess says they'll keep her through Sunday.

HENRY: Why do you want -- ? Why do you think it's necessary to go up and - ?

HENRY: I'd like to talk with her, make sure she's okay, and that she understands why we didn't take the baby.

HENRY: I'm sure she understands that.

JEAN: Don't you think we ought to finish it with her? What's the current usage? Don't you think a little -- what's the word --? A noun, begins with "K"?

HENRY: "Closure"?

JEAN: Exactly. Don't you think a little "closure" is in order?

HENRY: Maybe.

JEAN: I told Tess I'd like to go up.

HENRY: What'd she say?

JEAN: She didn't know what to say. She seemed surprised. She'd have to consult with a lot of different people at the agency, and DCFS, and the hospital.

HENRY: They won't let you meet the baby, will they?

JEAN: I don't think I want to meet him. I mean, how could I look into his face and tell him we had someone else in mind. I can't do that. How's that for cowardice?

HENRY: No.

JEAN: He's just waiting for someone. Lying there, looking around, waiting for the pay-off.

HENRY: It's not --
[She puts her head down. Henry pulls her into his arms. He is quiet. He feels her grief before he hears it. He looks miserably at the ceiling. Then in an unsteady bass, he sings:]
"O, COME ALL YE FAITHFUL
JOYFUL AND TRIUMPHANT
O, COME YE, O, COME YE
TO BETHLEHEM
COME AND BEHOLD HIM
　　　　　[His voice trails off.]
BORN THE. . .

[There is a silence, and then the lights fade to black.]

ACT III

SCENE 1

[July, 1991. Dr. Helen Arbaugh's tasteful inner office. There is a desk and a few assorted chairs. Lights come up to full as Arbaugh enters.]

DOCTOR: Sorry I'm late. *[She picks up the phone.]*

RADEMACHER: I just got here myself.

DOCTOR: Good.

RADEMACHER: Helen, we need about --

DOCTOR: Hang on, Viv. *[Into the phone:]* Effie, send them in.

RADEMACHER: Not yet, Helen.

LAURENCE: They've been waiting forty-five minutes, Viv.

RADEMACHER: A three minute discussion, Helen. Let's put up a united front.

DOCTOR: Oh, I think we can sort through it without a plan, Viv. This woman seems really rather extraordinary. Have you been reading Laurence's reports?

RADEMACHER: I have. She may be a bit of a nut case, Helen.

DOCTOR: Why on earth do you say that?

RADEMACHER: This child does not belong to her. Still, she visits every day. What person in their right mind -- ?
                    [Jean, Henry, and Franny enter.]

44

JEAN *[Innocently]*: I'm sorry. Am I interrupting? She told us we could come in.

LAURENCE: Is she interrupting, Viv?

RADEMACHER: Not at all. Hello there.

DOCTOR *[Turning to the three newcomers]:* Come in. I'm Helen Arbaugh, Robin's physician.

JEAN: I'm Jean Farrell.

DOCTOR: Nice meeting you, Jean. I know you and Laurence have met. Do you know Mrs. Rademacher?

JEAN: No, I don't.

RADEMACHER: Vivien Rademacher, administration.

JEAN: Oh! *[She shakes Viv's hand.]* Nice to meet you.

DOCTOR: If you don't mind, Vivien asked if she could join us this afternoon.

JEAN: Not at all. This is my husband, Henry, and our friend, Franny Stornant.
　　　[Henry and Franny shake hands with the doctor.]

DOCTOR: A pleasure. Vivien Rademacher.

RADEMACHER: Hello.

JEAN: Laurence, you don't know my husband, Henry.

HENRY *[Extending his hand]*: I've heard a lot about you.

LAURENCE: Likewise.

JEAN: And my friend, Franny Stornant.

LAURENCE [Offering his hand]: Mrs. Stornant.

JEAN: I was hoping --

DOCTOR [Picks up the phone again]: Did Effie offer you a cup of coffee?

JEAN: She did. No thanks.

DOCTOR: Forgive me. I'm a slave to it. [Into the phone:] Yes. And coffee. Ten minutes ago.

RADEMACHER: Mrs. Farrell, you have -- you've set a certain precedent, Mrs. Farrell. Much as we admire what seems to be your intent, we just need to get a few things clear. There are some legal matters that come into question concerning your visits.

LAURENCE: Which don't necessarily take into account what's best for the child.

RADEMACHER: I'm certain that's not so, but nonetheless --

DOCTOR: Let's back up a little. We'll get to all this, Viv. Mrs. Farrell, first, you wanted to ask me some questions about the baby's condition?

JEAN: Yes, I did.

DOCTOR: What do you want to know?

JEAN: He seems so uncomfortable. Isn't there anything more to be done for him?

DOCTOR: I'm afraid not much.

HENRY: We've been told he's not going to make it.

DOCTOR: The prognosis is extremely poor.

JEAN: There's supposed to be some kind of surgery you can do in cases like his?

DOCTOR: We did it.

JEAN: It didn't work?

DOCTOR: Robin was born via emergency C-section on the morning of June 6th, correct?

JEAN: Yes.

DOCTOR: His physicians at Silver Cross Hospital diagnosed severe hydrocephalia. He was flown from Joliet to Chicago that same afternoon.

JEAN: Right.

DOCTOR: We confirmed the original diagnosis. Hydrocephalia is caused by a defect in the membrane that is supposed to absorb cerebrospinal fluid. As a result, fluid collects in the cranium. This condition can also be caused by a tumor, and sometimes we see it happen after surgery to correct spina bifida.

JEAN: Yes.

DOCTOR: I operated on Robin to determine one thing. If the fluid in his head had been clean, then I would have installed a small tube under the skin, called a shunt. The tube is designed to carry excess water from the brain to the abdominal cavity, a place where the body may get rid of it. In Robin's case, the fluid was contaminated with debris. We did not implant the shunt. All that was left for us to do was to close him up, and make him as comfortable as possible.

JEAN: Debris? What does that mean? What are you talking about -- debris -- ?

DOCTOR: Foreign material.

JEAN: What kind of foreign material?

DOCTOR: Bone splinters from the cranium, and brain matter.

JEAN: I see.

HENRY: Chances are he's severely retarded, then?

DOCTOR: Yes.

JEAN: So you can't install a - what did you say? A shunt?

DOCTOR: Correct.

JEAN: It would get clogged.

DOCTOR: That's right. In order to keep the tube clear, we'd have had to perform major brain surgery every couple of weeks. There would certainly be infection, and other complications too numerous to mention.

JEAN: I see.

DOCTOR: That's the problem we faced. There was no one around at the time to steer us in another direction. Even so, I'm convinced we made the right decision.

JEAN: You mean you may have attempted to put in the shunt if a parent had insisted?

DOCTOR: It's possible, though it wouldn't have --

JEAN *[Suddenly up close and personal]*: That's what I meant,

Hal. He fell through the cracks in the transfer from Emma to us.

RADEMACHER: We do not allow our patients to fall through cracks, Mrs. Farrell. Dr. Arbaugh and the staff at the hospital are engaged in saving lives. We do everything in our power to--

LAURENCE: Relax, Vivien.

RADEMACHER: I beg your pardon?

LAURENCE: Relax. Nobody's gonna sue.

RADEMACHER: Laurence, you were invited to this meeting as a courtesy --

DOCTOR: Have you been designated his next of kin, Mrs. Farrell?

JEAN: No. Why do you ask?

DOCTOR: Just wondering who is in charge, that's all.

JEAN *[Regretfully]*: It's not me. Emma Miller is still his next of kin.

RADEMACHER: Are you trying to gain custody of the child?

HENRY: No. She's not. That's out of the question. Our agency has advised us to drop the adoption proceedings.

RADEMACHER: Then Emma Miller will remain the legal guardian? *[Disappointed]* I see. Mrs. Farrell, if that's the case, I'm not sure that it's right for you to have access to this baby. It could be harmful to both of you.

HENRY: That's what I'm wondering, too.

LAURENCE: Vivien, you're not on the floor. It won't do any harm. It's only for another couple of weeks.

JEAN: Why? What happens in a couple of weeks?

LAURENCE: They're trying to find a bed for him at Miserecordia, Jean. They think it will be about two more weeks before they can get him in.

RADEMACHER: The expenses of a special care unit are phenomenal, I'm sure you understand. Miss Miller, the legal guardian, is relying on state funds, which makes Robin's stay here untenable.

JEAN: What's Miserecordia?

LAURENCE: It's a home for individuals with special needs, run by the Sisters of the Sacred Heart.

RADEMACHER: It's a wonderful place, Mrs. Farrell. The sisters stress giving each child or adult the most normal life possible.

JEAN: Where is it?

LAURENCE: About thirty miles south of here.

JEAN: Thirty miles <u>south?</u>

LAURENCE: So, what's the harm, Vivien? Give them two more weeks.

RADEMACHER: I understand, believe me, Laurence, but technically, Mrs. Farrell had permission to visit the baby only once, over a week ago, on June 22nd. She's been back every day since. Your charts say that she cycles his arms and legs, and massages him.

LAURENCE: Yeah. It's pretty abusive stuff.

RADEMACHER: He is attached to a heart and lung monitor, is he not?

DOCTOR: It's standard procedure, Viv. I see no harm in a little exercise or massage.

RADEMACHER: Fine. However, the birth mother, Emma Miller, could come down mighty hard on this hospital if anything should--

JEAN: She won't.

LAURENCE: She doesn't come around anymore, Vivien. She wants Mrs. Farrell here.

HENRY: If something does go wrong, and you're at fault, Jean, she could take us to court.

JEAN: Henry, you met Emma! What are you talking about?

HENRY: I met her twice. She's sweet, but she told us herself she has no money, and no means of support.

JEAN: Jesus Christ.

LAURENCE: Vivien, cut to the chase. Are you going to terminate Mrs. Farrell's visiting privileges, or what?

RADEMACHER: I think it's a matter that needs serious examination. Mrs. Farrell, we do have volunteers who come to rock the babies three evenings a week, but they go through a training course, which you have not had.

LAURENCE: She doesn't need it. And the volunteers won't go near a baby like Robin. *[To Jean:]* They like the midgets.

RADEMACHER: According to our insurance underwriters -- I mean, I hate to be the one here who --

JEAN: Robin needs more than three evenings --

RADEMACHER: I know he does. I know he does, dear. So does every baby on the floor. But it's my job to protect both the children and this hospital. I know how you must feel. I know you've come to care for Robin, but we have the welfare of many children to consider. You do understand if there was anything more we could do for Robin, we'd bend every effort to it, don't you?

JEAN: Yes.

RADEMACHER: And you do understand that procedure here is strictly regulated by federal and state law, by private insurance carriers, by the Board of Directors.

JEAN: Yes. I do. Can I see him, or not?

RADEMACHER: Helen?

DOCTOR: Don't look at me, Viv. It's fine with me.

LAURENCE: And I'm game.
           [Rademacher shoots him a look.]
Not that anyone is asking.

RADEMACHER *[At last, to Jean]*: You can see him this afternoon, but I have to take this issue to committee. It's possible I may need to bring it before the Board. As I said, we're in new territory. We need to take it slowly.

LAURENCE: Naturally, since time is of the essence.

[Vivien opens her mouth to speak again.]

DOCTOR: Okay, thanks, Vivien. Thank you. You can go ahead. Laurence, thank you, you'd better get back to the floor.

RADEMACHER: I'm sorry, Mr. and Mrs. Farrell.
[She exits.]

HENRY: We understand. You've been very kind.

LAURENCE *[To Jean]*: I'll see you in a few minutes, then.

JEAN: Yes.

LAURENCE: Wanna hold him?

JEAN: Sure.

LAURENCE: I'll find Mary Jo. I have a surprise for you.

JEAN: What?

LAURENCE: See you upstairs. *[He exits.]*

DOCTOR: Is there anything else you wanted to ask me?

JEAN: I was going to ask if my husband and my friend could meet Robin this afternoon, just for a few minutes. Maybe I'd better not press it.

DOCTOR: It's fine with me. I'll waylay Vivien, and see if I can get her to go along with it.

HENRY: I don't know, Jean. Maybe it would be better if we didn't.

JEAN: Henry, just for a few minutes.

HENRY: I really don't want to get into legal difficulties with this hospital.

DOCTOR *[Looks from Jean to Henry]:* I don't sense a united front here.

HENRY: No, you don't.

DOCTOR: If you want me to intervene on your behalf, just say the word. Actually, I'm with Laurence. I think it does the baby good to have someone with a personal investment visiting each day. Why don't you just take a few minutes here to talk it over in private? Let me know what you want to do. In the mean time, I'll hunt down Effie and that cup of coffee, okay?

JEAN: Thank you.

[Lights come slowly up on Mary Jo, at the isolette, as they go down on the office.]

MARY JO: You're late.

DOCTOR: Take your time. Whatever you decide to do is fine.

JEAN: Thanks.
   [The doctor exits. Jean senses the resistance around her.]
So, now what?

HENRY: My mind is gone.

MARY JO: I've been waiting for you.

HENRY: I need a drink.

MARY JO: Major victory. They're putting him back on the bottle.

   [Jean picks up her bag and heads for the isolette]

SCENE 2

[The hospital. Later that day.]

JEAN: When?

MARY JO: Two o'clock this afternoon.

JEAN: All right!
[She approaches the crib quietly.]
Now, steady on, Babe, it's just me. How are you today?

MARY JO: So far, so good.

JEAN: Whoa, my little short stop. It fits, what do you know!
Wait a minute. Where is it? It's gone!

MARY JO: It's ancient history.

JEAN: The dreaded tube is gone! *[To Robin:]* Hey, there's a
profile for ya. Zowie.

MARY JO: Laurence took it out at 10:30. He's waiting for you,
too.

JEAN: He said he had a surprise.

MARY JO: Are you gonna be around at two o'clock?

JEAN: Yes.

MARY JO: The two o'clock feeding is yours.

JEAN: You're kidding.

MARY JO: I'm straight.

JEAN: Yay, Robin! How about that? He looks happy.

55

MARY JO: How can you tell?

JEAN: I don't know, really. That's a good question. His face is relaxed. You're doing great today, pal.
[Jean turns to her bag and rummages.]

MARY JO *[By way of explanation to Franny]*: He usually throws up when he first sees her. He gets those little arms and legs wheeling, and next thing you know, barf city. You're Franny?

FRANNY: Yes.

JEAN: I'm sorry, Mary Jo. Sorry. Yes, this is my friend, Franny Stornant.

MARY JO *[Extending her hand, Franny takes it.]*: It's good to see you. I've heard a lot about you.

FRANNY: Nice to meet you, too.

JEAN: She may have permission to be here, I don't know.

MARY JO: And I don't care. I'm just glad you made it.
[To Jean:]
Laurence wasn't sure. We thought Henry might -- we put him in the Cubs uniform just in case --

JEAN *[To Franny]*: Don't be shy. Come on. Come over here.
[Pulling back the covers]
There he is. There's my pal.

FRANNY *[In her years at the birthing center, she has not been privy to this.]* Sweet God.

JEAN: Say hello. Here's Franny, babe. Isn't she pretty?

FRANNY *[Still looking at the baby]*: Oh, Jean.

JEAN: What?

FRANNY: He's little.

JEAN: I know. Hey, you're doing great, pal.

FRANNY: He's -- he's just--

JEAN *[Proudly]*: I told you.

FRANNY: Hello, little baby.

[Jean produces a Walkman.]

MARY JO: What are you gonna do?

JEAN: I thought I'd play him some music.

MARY JO: No, come on.

JEAN: These sirens must drive him nuts.

FRANNY: Jean, do you think that's a good idea?

MARY JO: What've you got?

JEAN: I wanted something lyrical and simple. After due consideration, I think I'm going to go with Perlman and Domingo.

MARY JO *[Wrinkling her face, as she looks at the cassette cover]*: These are two geeks in open collars and sports jackets. Are you sure?

JEAN: I'm sure, Mary Jo.

MARY JO: They look like a couple of Tony Bennett wanna-bes.

JEAN: Mary Jo, I'm only going to say this once: get some professional help. Soon. *[Turning to the baby:]* All right now, look. See this? Walkman. What you are about to hear is food for your soul.

MARY JO: You should get him some Nirvana. "Smells Like Teen Spirit."

JEAN: Thanks for your input, Mary Jo, but I think it's crucial that we limit it to music that won't fry the few brains they say he has left.

MARY JO: He's a kid. He's gonna hate this stuff. Trust me.

JEAN: Let's find out.

FRANNY: Jean, he may be too fragile for something like this.

JEAN: Franny's not the first person to underestimate you, Robin. Don't take it personally. *[To Robin:]* I'm going to adjust this over your ears. *[She reaches in, and immediately encounters a problem she hadn't anticipated.]* Oh, no. Mama's an idiot.

MARY JO: Put it under his chin.

JEAN: And Mary Jo is a genius.

MARY JO: Tell Laurence.

JEAN: Volume is cool. Now, holler, kiddo, if it's too much. Raise a hand, kick a leg, spit up; I don't know. Give a sign, okay? *[She turns it on, and waits, watching him with intent.]*

[Sound: The audience finally gets a break from the beeps and whines. They hear the first strains of Toselli's "Serenata". The women cannot hear, so they watch. Mary Jo leans in.]

MARY JO: Is he dead?

JEAN: Robin?

MARY JO: Wow!

JEAN: Do you think he's okay?

[They see something in his manner, a sigh or an intake of breath.]

MARY JO:	**JEAN**:
Holy shit!	Good God!

FRANNY: I don't believe it.

MARY JO: Zone, baby, zone.

JEAN: That Perlman and Domingo, huh?

MARY JO: Jean, I went to the hospital library. I was looking around, and I found this. *[She hands Jean a photocopy of an article. Jean sits in the rocker, loosens her hospital gown, and begins to read. Mary Jo turns back to Franny at the crib.]* It's probably not my business, but I know she's not getting much support. I mean, as long as she comes anyway, somebody ought to be holding out a little hope.

FRANNY: Yes.

MARY JO: *[To the baby]*: Whuz up, Gee? How's my bud? That's right. Go with the beat, Babe. *[To Franny:]* How's Tom?

FRANNY *[Staring at her for a moment]*: I beg your pardon?

MARY JO: You have a son Tom? Stockbroker? Six-foot something?

FRANNY: Yes.

MARY JO: I could do with a six-foot stockbroker, let me tell you. I suppose he's also a nice guy.

FRANNY: He's swell.

MARY JO: Didn't he marry somebody with a crazy name?

FRANNY: That would be Bouie. *[Pronounced "Boo-ee"]*

MARY JO: Bouie.

JEAN *[Glancing up from her reading]*: I guess I talk about you a little.

FRANNY: I guess you do.

MARY JO: What kind of mother would name her daughter Bouie?

FRANNY: I believe it stands for Bernadine.

MARY JO: Bernadine! What kind of a mother would --?

FRANNY: A mother with a mother named Bernadine, I think.

MARY JO: Is she like her name?

FRANNY: Which one?

MARY JO: <u>Either</u> one.

FRANNY: Yes.

MARY JO: We're not fond of Bouie-slash-Bernadine, are we?

FRANNY: Oh, I don't know. Maybe we're just a little too fond of the six-foot stockbroker.

MARY JO *[To the baby]*: Are you lookin' at me, goomba-loomba? Smile, Robin. Smile.
>*[She reaches in and tickles him.]*

Geech, geech, geech, geech, geech! *[Nothing.]* You're hopeless, you know that?

JEAN *[Finishing the article]*: This is incredible.

MARY JO: I thought you'd like it.

JEAN *[Transfixed, she reads aloud]*: Listen to this, Franny: "While many hydrocephalic children have neurological problems, some are normal. Recently, British neurosurgeon John Lorber examined a number of people with severe untreated hydrocephalus - up to 95% of their brain tissue had been replaced by fluid. He reported startling findings: over half of the severely hydrocephalic individuals he examined had normal IQ's and were functioning well in society. One man was a university honors graduate in mathematics!"
>*[She is excited.]*

That's him. That's Robin.

FRANNY: Severe, <u>untreated</u> hydrocephalus?

JEAN: There's a chance his IQ is normal?

MARY JO: Fifty-fifty, according to the Brit.

JEAN: Wow.

MARY JO: I thought you'd like it.

JEAN: Why didn't Arbaugh tell me about this study?

MARY JO: Maybe she doesn't know. I had to do a little digging. Besides, most people see a child like this, and think it would be mercy if he died.

61

FRANNY: Surely, not the child's surgeon.

MARY JO: Well. You wouldn't think so.

JEAN: Thank you, Mary Jo, thank you.

MARY JO: Consider me your spin doctor.

JEAN *[To Franny]*: What do you think?

FRANNY: I'd want to talk it over with Doctor Arbaugh.

JEAN: So, I will. *[She joins Franny at the crib.]* You should have seen him a few days ago. He's improved.

FRANNY: He's awfully content at the moment.

MARY JO: I'm gonna have to get me some Perlman and Domingo.

JEAN: You don't know what you're missing.

MARY JO: Are they even close to the Top One Hundred?

JEAN: It depends on the Top One Hundred you're talking about.

MARY JO: The kid don't smile.

JEAN: The kid don't have much to smile about. Now, Mary Jo, I want to learn how to pick him up. Just me. Like you guys do.

MARY JO: No. Not me. I don't.

JEAN: I thought--

MARY JO: Oh, no. I'm a notch above a candy-striper, okay? Nurse's aide: I do diapers and some medication, just to give you

an idea?

JEAN: Who _does_ pick him up? Laurence?

MARY JO: He prefers two of us, but I've seen him do it by himself. I'll get Laurence. *[Mary Jo starts to go, but thinks better of it.]* Don't _do_ anything. I'll be right back.

JEAN: Trust me.

MARY JO: I've seen you in action.

JEAN: Not till I've had a lesson, believe me.

[Enter Laurence.]

LAURENCE *[addressing Mary Jo]*: Where _are_ you? Why can I never _find_ you?

MARY JO: I was just looking for you.

LAURENCE: What a marvelous coincidence, then. Lucky us. Kelly Davis needs aspirating.

MARY JO: Okay.

LAURENCE: She stopped breathing ten minutes ago.

MARY JO *[To Jean]*: He's kidding. Though she _is_ stuffed up. Mrs. Farrell would like a lesson in picking up the baby. Like you do, sometimes, alone.

LAURENCE: Okay. I'll see to it. Chop, chop, Mary Jo.
[Mary Jo exits.]
There goes the most indolent creature on the face of the earth. "Beulah, peel me a grape," doesn't begin to describe it.

JEAN: I wouldn't say so.

LAURENCE: You know something I don't?

JEAN: She keeps herself busy.

LAURENCE: Mrs. Stornant! How lovely. Your follow-through is admirable. Where's the mister?

FRANNY: He had to go back to work.

LAURENCE: He's a free-lance writer, isn't he?

JEAN: That's the party-line, Laurence, okay?

LAURENCE: I love a party. We do have clearance for this little visit?

JEAN: From Doctor Arbaugh. We weren't able to locate Mrs. Rademacher.

LAURENCE: I didn't hear that second part, okay?

JEAN: What second part?

LAURENCE: As long as we understand each other. Now, what? You want to pick the kid up?

JEAN: And make it to the rocker, each of us in one piece.

LAURENCE: Okay. Here's what you do. Get your right hand under his back and hips.

JEAN: Now?

LAURENCE: Or I could meet you here a week from Tuesday.

JEAN: All right, all right. *[She moves in to the isolette]* Oh, God.

LAURENCE: Stop imagining things, okay? Just follow my directions.

JEAN: Right.

LAURENCE: Take the fingers of your left hand, and start exploring the nape of his neck. Wait, let me disconnect the monitors.
[He looks into the crib for the first time.]
What the hell is that?

JEAN: It's a Walkman.

LAURENCE *[Truly stumped, he lets out a breath, and scratches the back of his neck.]* Peter, Paul & Mommy?

JEAN: Would that be better?

LAURENCE: It's good. I can't believe you found it necessary to hook him up to yet another machine.

JEAN: This one is different.

LAURENCE: What are you playing for him?

JEAN: Perlman and Domingo.

LAURENCE: "Danny Boy"?

JEAN: Toselli's "Serenata".

LAURENCE: Nice. Get it off him.

JEAN: Okay.

LAURENCE: Lovely choice, though.

[Jean starts maneuvering.]

JEAN: So, I'm exploring the nape of his neck with my fingers.

LAURENCE: Move them up his head til you feel the bones of his skull. There's sort of a rigid bowl there.

JEAN: Got it.

LAURENCE: And you've got his back and hips?

JEAN: Yes, I think so.

LAURENCE: If your chair is ready --

FRANNY *[Making quick adjustments]*: It is.

LAURENCE: More pressure on the bone of his head than on his back. Lift away.

JEAN: Jesus!

LAURENCE: I'm right here. Lift away.

JEAN *[Trusting him, she lifts the child, and makes her way toward the rocker]*: Jesus God.

FRANNY: You're doing fine.

LAURENCE: He's top-heavy, but you knew that.

JEAN: I can't sit.

LAURENCE: You can.

JEAN: I'll drop him.

LAURENCE: Sit!

JEAN: I'm going to drop him.

FRANNY: No, you're not.

LAURENCE: You're going to sit.
                    [Quietly]
Sit down, Jean.
    [She does. They look at one another, full of triumph.]
Ta-dah! That's all there is to it.

JEAN: My life passed before my eyes, do you know that?

LAURENCE: Think how he must have felt.

JEAN: Poor gummy.

LAURENCE: You're okay.

JEAN: What's that?

LAURENCE: You're good.

JEAN: Okay. Good.

LAURENCE: I've got an enema to attend to.

JEAN: By all means --

LAURENCE *[To the baby]*: Well, you're the cat that got the cream, aren't you? *[To Jean:]* Holler when you want to make the return trip.

JEAN: Yeah, well, don't go too far.

LAURENCE: Aisle Three, kiddo. *[He starts to go, and remembers]* Did she tell you? She told you, didn't she?

JEAN: Yes!

LAURENCE: The bitch!

JEAN: And the IV is gone.

LAURENCE: Of course. Silly me. I'll meet you at two.
                    [He's gone.]

JEAN: You there, Fran?

FRANNY: Just pulling up a chair. *[A beat]* Sorry.

JEAN: What?

FRANNY: I apologize.

JEAN: Why?

FRANNY: Never mind. I'm here now.

JEAN: Oh. You know, you might want to bring Scott out of hiding one of these days. I'll roast a chicken or something.

FRANNY: You don't have to --

JEAN: A roast chicken doesn't necessarily mean I'll be his bosom buddy. Just an attempt at objectivity.

FRANNY: Thank you.

JEAN: I'm holding my child.

FRANNY: I see.

JEAN *[Turning her attention to the baby.]*: Let's see now, Robin, you've made some progress with the rash from hell. The feeding tube is gone. How about that? And you're going to have an unparalleled feast at two. When the time comes, suck, Robin, like you do with Mommy's finger. Laurence won't take any guff, and he'll be up your nose with the dreaded rubber hose, if you don't suck. I mean it. I'm gonna start with your

68

head instead of your feet today, okay? And here's what I want
you to think about: since they're not going to do any more for
you, by way of surgery, to relieve this pressure, you're going to
have to start doing for yourself, darlin'.

[Massaging his head, and telling him a campfire story.]
My dad was a pack rat, too. He managed to store every bit of
saran wrap, string, and aluminum foil from the time my
grandmother first started packing his lunches back in 1932. He
had every knickknack anybody ever gave him, including, but not
limited to, four mugs depicting women in evening gowns; the
more you drank, the less they were wearing, okay? -- just to
give you an idea of the "debris and foreign material" that was in
Grandpa's life?

FRANNY: Surely, you jest.

JEAN *[To Franny]*: He actually had a one-horse power outboard
motor that Evinrude stopped making in nineteen-fifty. *[Back to
the story:]* His hall closet bulged with golf clubs and tennis
rackets, and rolls of toilet paper he got on sale at K-Mart. Only
the truly brave, with ropes securely tied round their waists,
descended the cellar stairs, for the basement was so burdened
that one could only make it to the washer-dryer by negotiating a
treacherous, winding path past stacks of yellowing newspapers,
lava lamps, and bamboo hat racks whose arms reached out to
snag at your clothes and clutch at your hair. People went into
that basement to add the fabric softener, and were never heard
from again. We pleaded with your Grandpa to get help, to call
Am-Vet, or the Salvation Army. We begged him to understand
that with one carelessly tossed match, he would create an
inferno, the likes of which, Dante would be hard pressed to
describe. But he refused to listen. Time and again, he
admonished us with one simple phrase, that left us bewildered
and silent: "Waste not, want not," he would say. Then, just
when we thought it was too late, a miracle happened. He
retired, and decided to move to Florida. In one all out, ride-it-
to-hell rummage sale, over four consecutive afternoons, he made
forty-seven hundred dollars, Robin. And as he bid farewell to

the last of the mugs, and the dressers, and the car-vacs; when his house was clear, and clean, and empty, we watched one magical afternoon in autumn, as he turned into a beautiful snow bird with white wings, a set of golf clubs, and a tee-shirt that read: "Nixon's the one, and Agnew's another one." And he flew up into the gray and white sky, turned south, and soared from view. The moral of this story is: if you don't need it, chuck it. You're like Grandpa, only you save water. Southern California could profit by your example. But, take it easy. You're still very small. No need to take on our sins just yet. You're a baby. *[With deeper intent]* You're my Robin. If you're thirsty, if you need water, I'll know it, and I'll give you a drink, okay?

FRANNY *[Slipping from the chair]*: Maybe I should leave you two alone for a while.

HENRY *[From the dark]*: It would take everything you've got to raise an absolutely perfect baby, let alone a baby who lies flat on his back twenty-four hours a day.

[Cross-fade begins]

FRANNY: I'll be out in the hall.

HENRY: What would you do about the university? You can't leave a child like Robin with some teen-aged baby-sitter. You can't put him in a normal daycare setting.

[Franny crosses into Arbaugh's office.]

SCENE 3

[As the lights fade on Jean, she picks up the baby, almost easily, and returns him to the crib. She attaches the machines and restores the Walkman.]

JEAN: Let it go. Let it go for Mama.

FRANNY: Maybe it would be best if I waited in the hall, Henry.

HENRY: No, Franny, stay a minute.

FRANNY: It's for the two of you to decide.

HENRY: You've raised a child of your own.

FRANNY: That hardly makes me --

HENRY: This baby needs round the clock care.

JEAN *[Approaching the office]*: Honey, I know that.

HENRY: He needs a trained nurse on the scene. He needs special handling, and special medication.

JEAN: I know. When did I ever say I was going to bring him home?

HENRY: You don't have to say it.

JEAN: Maybe Emma would help. Maybe she'd take room and board, in exchange for --

HENRY: You've lost your mind. Emma lives on welfare with her alcoholic father and her two-year-old son. Look, the agency is still in our corner. They'll find us another child. It means waiting again, that's all.

JEAN: I don't want to wait any more. I don't have to wait. I have a child right here to look after. Okay, Emma is out. I know it's crazy. But, I can find a way to make it work, if you will just give me a chance. Maybe he can't live with us, but why are you so against my seeing him? Don't you trust me, Hal?

71

HENRY: It's not a question of--

JEAN: Do you <u>trust</u> me? Do you think I will look after our best interest? I'm not saying bring him home and raise him. I know you're against that idea.

HENRY: But, you're not, Jean. You'll figure out a way.

JEAN: So, now I'm a conniver?

HENRY: I don't know.

JEAN: Well, that's interesting.

HENRY: Just get yourself above the situation. Have the courage to mourn.

JEAN: He's not dead! He's alive and kicking about fifty yards from here. He won't contaminate you.

HENRY: What did you say?

JEAN: We made a commitment to Emma that we would look after him from the moment he was born.

HENRY: Don't you dare do this to me! I <u>never</u> committed to this child! It was always understood I would only accept a healthy infant. When they did the home study, I said, no physical handicaps.

JEAN: And if I had given birth to him, what then? Would you still be walking out on me today?

HENRY: That is a pointless thing to ask, because you did not give birth to him, Jean. I can't tell you what my reaction would be if you had. I really don't know. What I do know is that in this particular situation, I have a choice. Nothing you can say will trick me out of making it.

JEAN: Trick you?

FRANNY: He's thinking of you, Jean, of what your life will be like --

JEAN: Well, cut it out. Do me a favor, and stop thinking of me. I don't want you to think of me.

FRANNY: He needs a mother's care. It's up to his mother -

JEAN: Who is mother now, Franny? Who's his mother?

HENRY: Emma!

JEAN: Emma's out of the picture. That's not the legality, I know, but it's the reality. He doesn't have one soul to care for him, or to intercede on his behalf.
 [To Henry, in a more reasonable tone.]
But, Hal, I beg you. Let me see him. Just don't make an issue of it.

HENRY: Don't you remember how it was? I thought we were losing our minds the day he was born.

JEAN: We did lose them, but we got them back. Minds are like boomerangs.

HENRY: You have no recollection of that day, do you?

JEAN: Look, I'll keep you out of it.

HENRY: You really don't, do you?

FRANNY: No, she doesn't.

HENRY: There is no future for us here. The boy is dying. Why do you want to grab on just as the people who know best have told you it's time to let go?

73

JEAN *[She finds her position]*: I'm going to visit today, and again tomorrow, and the day after that, until they send him to Miserecordia. Then I will visit him at Miserecordia. Henry, you talk about the pain we felt, and it's true, we did. It's pain I gather you're still feeling. I'm not. Haven't you noticed? All gone. He did it. You're right, you do have a choice: you can come with me, and meet him, or you can go home, and hang on to your precious pain. I'd like your blessing, Hal, but if I don't get it, that's fine, too.

HENRY: During the course of our marriage, I've watched you invite loners and orphans on holidays; I've seen you feed every stray cat in the neighborhood; you'll give your last buck to the winos on Morse Avenue. It's a thing with you, Jean; makes you feel good. And you get paid back in spades whenever you do some bleeding heart thing. And it never really costs you much. It's a way to congratulate your self on your own goodness. It's a way to maintain that Pollyanna Catholicism that you have perfected to an art form, my girl. But, I'm telling you, you're in very deep water this time. This time it's different. My best judgment is that you have no idea what you're doing. If Robin survives, he'll languish his whole life long, and I will watch you struggle to fulfill some kind of promise that no one in the world expects you keep: not me, not our family, not our friends, not the agency, not even Emma. If he dies, we'll have another round of misery like we've had for the last month. And Jean? I don't know how you begin to imagine you are capable of taking it. Even if you can take it, and believe me, I'm not thinking of you at the moment, I can't take it! Although you haven't noticed, although you don't remember, I'm part of this. I'm the one who picks up the pieces around here: I'm the one who held you, and heard you, and fed you, and coaxed you to bed for nights on end..... You've asked for my blessing? Well, you can't have it. You can't have it.

[He exits.]

JEAN: We'll take a bus home.

FRANNY *[Picks up her bag.]*: I don't know, Jean. I think it's best if I go, too.

JEAN: Stay. Meet him. Meet Robin.

FRANNY: I think I'm with Henry on this one.

JEAN: You're on a roll lately, I'll tell you.

FRANNY: I know you think I've betrayed Sam, but how have I betrayed you?

JEAN: You're <u>leaving</u> me, like you left Sam. That's what betrayal is, Franny: desertion in time of need; proving false.

FRANNY: I don't really mind your judgment. The things I say to myself are far worse than anything you could ever say. What I do mind is the double-standard. You don't hold yourself accountable in the same way.

JEAN: Well, this is good. How so?

FRANNY: Have you looked at your husband lately? At the eyes, at the skin and bone? When did you last see him do one spontaneous thing? What you don't get, what you refuse to get, is that the one who leaves isn't necessarily the one who abandons. My husband abandoned me long ago. It took me years to see it, because we still shared the same house, two seemingly amiable souls, who hadn't really connected with one another in years. I left. In "abandoning" him, I've done us both a huge favor. Sam is alive again. How do you rationalize your abandonment of Henry? He's been with you every step of the way.

JEAN: You cannot compare your situation with ours. It's absurd.

FRANNY: You can't expect Henry to want to support Robin.

The man is forty-six years old. He has one shot at being a
father, and he wants it to be a joyful experience, not a tragedy.

JEAN: Yes? And?

FRANNY: Jean! You don't seriously believe raising Robin would
be a joyful experience?

JEAN: Well, you don't, that's clear.

FRANNY: Not every one is cut out to raise a child with special
needs. Henry said in all honesty he was not. You agreed to go
into this adoption together, knowing that. To force him to do
something against his nature, is also a betrayal.

JEAN: I am not forcing him to <u>do</u> anything. We have an
opportunity. I'm <u>asking</u> him to <u>look</u>. Meet Robin. Educate
himself a little. <u>Then</u> we'll come to a decision, which I will
abide by.

FRANNY: Henry has already come to that decision, for very
private reasons of his own. You refuse to understand that, or
even hear it. You're in love with Robin. And you don't want to
have to choose between your marriage and this child.

JEAN: I want them both.

FRANNY: You can't have both. That's the catch. You will
choose eventually, because your life will be a nightmare if you
don't. Dammit, Jean, over the years, I've heard in minute detail
what you want from motherhood. I'm privy to every secret wish
in your head. None of it has anything to do with this boy. This
boy will never walk. He'll never read. He'll never know his
numbers. Never chase a cat, or play baseball, or run down the
stairs on Christmas morning. There will be no idle chat around
the kitchen table, no laughter, no horseplay. He can't possibly
make his way in this world. Not <u>this</u> world. He'll never fall in
love, never know a woman, never bounce a child on his knee. I

am your friend. It seems to me the only thing I can <u>do</u> at this point is to try to stop you from making a terrible mistake, one which will not only ruin your marriage, but also your life. Your <u>life</u>, Jean.

JEAN *[With a litany of her own]*: Once, do you remember -- when I was going through all the surgeries and in vitros, when I was exhausted from the drugs and the needles and the schedules, when we didn't know where else to look for money or support, and you and every other old friend were busy with baby showers, the first day of school, Little League, the prom, and finally college applications; when I had had it up to here with the advice, and then the silence, and then the pity from each one of you, not to mention the image of self-indulgence I encountered in the mirror every morning; in an attempt to comfort me, you said, Franny, and I quote: "If you think the journey has been difficult for you, think what it must be like for the child who is trying to get to you." I laughed when you said it; it sounded so New Age. But, the terrible thing is, you were right! I look at Robin, and see evidence of a harrowing journey.

FRANNY: You don't think I meant this? I never meant this. I only meant to comfort -- I <u>do</u> remember, and in retrospect, it was a remark that was easy, and clever. I never meant for you to chain yourself to the first --

JEAN: Of course you didn't mean this. What kind of idiot would wish for a child with Robin's problems? I wish to God he was healthy! No one ever dreams of this! But, sometimes, this is what comes. In fifteen years of doing everything I can think of to bring a child into my life, this child is the one I've been given. And to my surprise, he's better than anything I <u>ever</u> dreamt. I know you think that's crazy, and so does Henry. Because you won't <u>look</u>, and if you <u>don't</u> look, you won't <u>get</u> it.

FRANNY: We're afraid for you. We love you.

JEAN: I know you do. But, do you think if I walked away from

77

him now, I could ever love you, or Henry, or anyone else, ever again? ... Do you really think I could live with myself -- seeing what he's been through, what he is still going through -- if I knew he'd found no love to make his journey worthwhile? You're frightened of Robin because you think he is "his problem". If you come with me, you will see past the deformity, I assure you, to the tremendous person he has had to become in one short month. I am so certain of this, that if you still don't get it, after you've spent an afternoon with him, I'll walk out of here, away from him for the last time, without one backward glance.

FRANNY: Jean --

JEAN: I'm extending a privilege to you. Don't mistake it for anything else.

FRANNY: [Beat] Okay.

[Franny and Jean stand blinking at one another.]

JEAN: What?

FRANNY: I said okay. Lead on. Let's go meet Robin.

[Without further ado, Jean picks up her things and leads Franny out of the room. Black-out.]

INTERMISSION

ACT IV

SCENE 1

[Place: Michigan's Asolbo River. It is a dark and stormy night. Dripping woods loom above and a gray, sullen lake lies in the distance. Henry and Sam are miserable. Henry huddles under a tarp to ward off the wet and cold. Their fishing gear lies nearby. Sam is attempting to light a fire with no success. Together the men have killed half a bottle of vodka.]

SAM: Birch bark, that's what we need. *[He attempts to light another wet match. Henry looks on with a mixture of thinly veiled pity and contempt.]*

HENRY: What's that you say?

SAM: We could get this fire going if we had birch bark. In a wet woods, you can always start a fire with birch bark. The Indians used it for everything. You can write letters on it. You can sew with it, lace up your moccasins with it. You can even build a canoe. The bark has petroleum in its skin, which makes it not only waterproof, but also flammable. It's a natural accelerant.

HENRY: That's wonderful.

SAM: Oh, yeah. Find yourself a piece of drenched birch bark, set a match to it, and you've got yourself a fire.

HENRY: It's white, isn't it, Sam? Birch bark?

SAM: That's right.

HENRY: Is that a birch over there? *[Indicating something in the distance.]*

SAM *[Sam looks up]:* Yes, it is. That's a yellow birch. The

79

Irish considered that particular kind of birch to be a bewitching tree. I think they called it the white lady of death. They actually believed the top branches could reach down and touch your soul. If it did that, you were a goner.

HENRY: Lots of birch bark right there, then.

SAM: That's a live tree, Henry. We'll pay a five hundred dollar fine if they catch us messing with a live tree. A birch is fragile; if it has open places in the skin, the insects get inside and kill it.

HENRY: Oh.

SAM: The wind plays havoc with it, too.

HENRY: Too bad.

SAM: But, even if that <u>was</u> a dead tree?

HENRY: Yeah?

SAM: We've got a helluva a lot of soggy matches here. Birch bark doesn't ignite all by itself.

HENRY: So, the subject of birch bark is pretty much a moot one.

SAM: Pretty moot. A doggone waste of breath, actually. Now, if I'd thought to bring along some steel wool, we could unravel a piece of it, and together with the flashlight batteries, get a spark going.

HENRY: But, you didn't think to bring steel wool?

SAM: No, I didn't. Even if I had, we'd still need a heck of a lot of --

TOGETHER: Birch bark.

SAM: It's your basic Catch 22. *[Indicating a bottle of vodka that Henry clutches to his side.]* Don't bogey that bottle.

HENRY *[Surrendering it]*: I'm going to remember what I've learned tonight. You never know when you'll get yourself stuck in the middle of a wet woods, in freezing weather, with night coming on.

SAM: It's handy information.

HENRY: It is. *[Beat]* However, strictly speaking, a Catch-22 it is not, Sam. If you're in the mood to split hairs, and what the fuck else do we have to do on a night like this? A Catch-22 is a situation where something desirable is unattainable because one of its requirements can never exist in the presence of some other of its requirements.

SAM: Say again?

HENRY: The lack of fire making tools is only really a Catch-22, if the necessary birch bark isn't available precisely because steel wool is, or vice versa.

SAM: Ah. I see. *[Silence]* Would the term SNAFU be more applicable?

HENRY: I believe I can allow it, yes.

SAM: Fine. Tell me this --

HENRY: Yes?

SAM: Jean puts up with you every day and every night, is that right?

HENRY: Essentially.

SAM: Wonderful woman.

HENRY: Patient woman, yes. Might I add that it is my sincere hope that the tranquility of your marriage to Franny did not rest on your fire-building abilities.

SAM: It did not.

HENRY: Good.

SAM: Goddamn Mount Pinatubo. It'll warm up tomorrow. But, hell, if it's warm, if it's cold, if we freeze our butts off, I'll still take the woods every time. I can finally breathe! Can you breathe?

HENRY: No problem so far.

SAM: How I ever came to believe a transfer to the New York office of Arthur Anderson was my destiny calling, I will never know. Anyway, my kid is married, my wife has fled the scene, and I am thinking about coming back here for good.

HENRY: Back to Michigan? What would you do?

SAM: Start my own accounting firm. I was raised in the woods.

HENRY: No kidding?

SAM: Hell, yes. My folks owned a lodge in Gaylord. This is home to me. I've come home! God! I love it here. There's no duplicity here. There's no room for liars here. You've gotta tough it out, know what I mean?

HENRY: Not exactly, Sam. My definition of roughing it has always involved a screen door of some kind.

SAM: You've never been camping?

HENRY: Hotels and boardwalks come strongly into play when I'm defining a really swell vacation. Give me white sand, a mai

tai, and some sun tan oil, and I am on vacation!

SAM: Why did you suggest camping, then?

HENRY: Was this my idea?

SAM: If memory serves.

HENRY: You're kidding! I don't know. I thought I could get you to meet me here. I know you like to camp.

SAM: Well, next time suggest the mai tai, sun tan oil thing.

HENRY: You got it.

SAM: *[He shakes his head. Humiliated.]* It's the kindness that's killing me. All the mushroom soup and tuna casseroles from the neighbor ladies, the endless analysis over drinks with well-meaning pals, and now this: Deliverance 2.

HENRY: It wasn't just for you. I needed to get away.

SAM: Yeah?

HENRY: Yeah.

SAM: I heard you guys are in trouble.

HENRY: It's a mess.

SAM: She really wants to bring that kid home?

HENRY: She really does.

SAM: If she does, then what? Will you leave?

HENRY: She wouldn't. She won't.

SAM: There's no telling what a woman will do, especially one who knows she's suckered your trust. You're a writer.

HENRY: Sometimes.

SAM: Then you know about the weakness in human nature. Women are the worst. Tell me about Franny, for example.

HENRY: I beg your pardon?

SAM: Quote somebody. Tell me I'm not crazy. Tell me the worst thing anybody ever wrote about a woman.

HENRY: Why would you want -- ?

SAM: Or women, in general. Let's throw caution to the wind, and just lump 'em all together, what do you say? Because, after seventeen years, I never thought I could hate her, but I do.

HENRY: Hate?

SAM: I financed that fucking birthing center of hers. It was the biggest mistake of my life. Once it took off, we were stuck. There was no considering a transfer out of that hell hole. She was in paradise. She was always so -- lah-de-dah, off to the theatre, galleries in Soho, concerts in Central Park. "Let's step over this inert body to get a better view of the Chrysler Building." Jesus Christ, if I'd had to hear her wax sentimental one more time about the fucking Chrysler building -- have you been to New York lately?

HENRY: What are you talking about?

SAM: Calcutta without the cows, that's what I'm talking about. Mass psychosis! I can hardly leave the house any more. From an airplane, it looks exactly like a malignant skin tumor.

HENRY: But I thought--

SAM: After all the years I suffocated in that pit for her sake, I lose my mind when I think of her with that jerk -- I think up tortures. I dream of murder.

HENRY: Whoa.

SAM: If one other person has hated a woman the way I hate Franny, I might survive. So tell me the worst. It was probably Shakespeare, wasn't it? Shakespeare could hate a woman, couldn't he?

HENRY: What?

SAM: Shakespeare could hate a woman.

HENRY: Yes.

SAM: Couldn't he?

HENRY: He could be venomous on the subject, yes.

SAM: What'd he say? Hit me with it! No holds barred!

HENRY: That's good. "No holds Bard." I like that.

SAM: Go ahead.

HENRY: Let me think. Well, there's <u>King Lear:</u>
> *[Scanning beautifully]*
> Behold yon simp'ring dame,
> Something, something
> Down from the waist they are something,
> Something, something
> But to the waist do the gods inherit,
> Beneath is all the fiend's.
> There's hell, there's darkness, there is the sulphurous
>   pit,
> Burning, scalding, something, something; fie, fie, fie!

SAM *[Who has stopped carefully laying matches to dry on a towel, in order that he may listen]:* "The sulphurous pit?" He actually said that?

HENRY: Takes your breath away, doesn't it?

SAM: That's some memory you got there. Something, something.

HENRY: Does that do it for you?

SAM: It comes pretty damn close. Doesn't <u>quite</u> say it, but it comes close.

HENRY: Then there's Yeats, who wrote about forgiveness.

SAM: Fuck him.

HENRY: Right.

[Cross-fade]

SCENE 2

[The hospital. Jean makes her way to the side of the isolette, where Mary Jo waits for her.]

MARY JO: Jean!

JEAN: Mary Jo, how's it going?

MARY JO: Fine!

JEAN *[Looking into the crib]:* What's he plugged into?

MARY JO: Green Chili Jam.

JEAN: Where's Humpty?

MARY JO: He hurled all over Humpty. Humpty pissed him off, that's all I can figure.

JEAN *[To Mary Jo]*: So, he's eating, then?

MARY JO: A record four ounces.

JEAN: Good boy.

MARY JO: Jean, we've got a situation on our hands.

JEAN: What's that? What do we have?

MARY JO: A bit of a situation. That's what I would call it: a situation. I can't say what kind of a situation until the L-man gets here. He'll come down on me like a ton of bricks if I explain about...

JEAN: The situation.

MARY JO: Right.

JEAN: Go get him.

MARY JO: Okay.

JEAN: I want to know.

MARY JO: Okay. *[Colliding with Laurence]*

LAURENCE: Did you tell her? Mary Jo, if you told her --

MARY JO: No, no, no. Go! Talk.

LAURENCE: Because if you told her --

MARY JO: Talk. Go.

JEAN: What is wrong with you people?

LAURENCE: Sit down.

JEAN *[Sitting]*: What is it? Tell me.

LAURENCE: Jean, something peculiar is going on, and, we're excited, which takes the Charles Grodin Understatement of the Week Award.

JEAN: What? What is it? What's going on?

LAURENCE: As you know, every Monday and Thursday morning, I weigh Robin, and measure the circumference of his head.

JEAN: Yes?

LAURENCE: This morning, I noticed he'd dropped six ounces when I weighed him, and I thought, here's an oddity. Then, when I measured his head, he'd lost seven centimeters. Somehow, between last Monday and today, he has found a way to rid himself of seven centimeters.

JEAN: Is that a lot?

LAURENCE: About three inches. A little fluctuation is normal, but this is -- a lot, yes. So, I looked up his birth records, and all told, he's lost eight and a half centimeters since he first came here a month and a half ago.

JEAN: What's happening to it? Where is it going?

LAURENCE: We're not sure. Somehow he's managing to flush it away.

MARY JO: Let's call a spade a spade. He's pissing it into his diapers.

JEAN: Is he?

LAURENCE: That appears to be the case, yes.

JEAN: What does Arbaugh say?

LAURENCE: She can't really explain it, either. It should not be happening.

MARY JO: It's a miracle!

LAURENCE: Mary Jo, let's try to stay on the same page.

MARY JO: How else do you explain it?

LAURENCE: I'll be happy to set you up with Arbaugh.

MARY JO: But, she can't explain it either.

JEAN: Is that true?
[Laurence nods. Jean is careful, but obviously radiant]
I knew he was smart ... I knew he was clever, but, I really had no idea he was a prodigy.

MARY JO: This proves it.

LAURENCE: Look, I can tell you that I haven't seen anything like this, but it's important for you to know--

JEAN: Can I pick him up?

LAURENCE: Uh -- sure. Mary Jo, you want to help me -- ?

JEAN: No, no. I'll get him. *[She rises, goes to the crib, and easily takes up the child.]* You clever, clever boy! You amazing shrinking thing, you! Are you practicing voodoo when I'm not here? *[She sits with him, and rubs his head tenderly.]* It's important that I know what?

LAURENCE: Well, it's important that you grasp the fact, that although we are stumped, it is what it is. It is only what it is. That's it. It's nothing more.

JEAN: Have you been reading Camus?

LAURENCE: What I mean to say is that it doesn't necessarily prove he's on the road to recovery. He could gain back this water any time.

JEAN: He could, but he won't.

LAURENCE: But, the other thing, Jean, is that they've found a bed for him at Miserecordia.

JEAN: When?

LAURENCE: Three days from now.

JEAN: Tell me exactly where this place is.

LAURENCE: About thirty or forty minutes south of here.

JEAN: Shit.

LAURENCE: How long does it take you to get here?

JEAN: About an hour and a half. It's the construction on Lake Shore Drive.

LAURENCE: So, we're talking two hours to Miserecordia, and two hours back.

MARY JO: The train is faster.

LAURENCE: What about your job?

JEAN: I'll take a sabbatical.

LAURENCE: You don't need to see him every day, either, Jean. You could come two or three times a week.

JEAN: I do have to see him every single day, and he has to see me. We can't afford a set-back.

LAURENCE: I can try to convince Arbaugh to hold off on the release. But, he's travel-worthy, and as long as the state is picking up the bill, old Viv will be breathing down my neck.

JEAN: This is absurd. Why are we discussing the empty bed at Miserecordia, when he has an empty bed ready for him at home? He has a bed, with bumpers, and soft quilts, and a zoo of stuffed animals that are fading with the wait. Why should I drive four hours every day, when I need only walk up a flight of stairs? The money I would spend on gas alone will pay for someone to come in and help me part time. Why are we sitting here talking like all of that does not exist?

LAURENCE: Do you really want an answer, or is this just oratory?

JEAN: Robin's coming home, that's all there is to it.

LAURENCE: And Henry? You gonna get him lobotomized or what?

JEAN: He has to agree. That's it.

LAURENCE: Not just for your sake, either. DCFS won't place even a child as needy as Robin in a home where there is strife.

MARY JO: Leave your husband.

JEAN: What?

MARY JO: Leave the bastard.

LAURENCE: Mary Jo!

MARY JO: DCFS places with lots of single parents.

LAURENCE: That's hardly the point.

MARY JO: He sounds like an ogre. I say leave him.

JEAN: Have I made him out to be an ogre?

MARY JO: Authentic dweeb.

LAURENCE: Mary Jo, are you on some sort of medication that I as your immediate supervisor ought to know about?

JEAN: Have I really made him out to be so bad?

MARY JO: The "iceman cometh." Some snowman guy.

LAURENCE: Mary Jo, are you, by any chance, and I shudder to think, referring to the play by Eugene O'Neill, entitled The Iceman Cometh?

MARY JO: Maybe.

LAURENCE: I have a certain admiration for you, Mary Jo. You smack up against great literature the way Jerry Ford used to hit doorways. In Eugene O'Neill's classic, The Iceman Cometh, Hickey is a notorious womanizer, who repeatedly cheats on his wife, and eventually kills her to spare her the pain of his indiscretions. Do you honestly see a parallel here?

MARY JO: Before I answer that?

LAURENCE: Yes?

MARY JO: Who's Jerry Ford?

LAURENCE: Shoot me.

JEAN: Laurence.

LAURENCE: Somebody pull the trigger.

JEAN: The problem is with me, do you understand?

MARY JO: No, it's not.

JEAN: Yes, it is.

LAURENCE: What? What are we talking about now?

JEAN: He could have had children of his own if it weren't for me. And yet, he's never complained. If I've misled you, Mary Jo, I apologize. My slightest wish has been his command. He's given me every single thing I ever wanted.

LAURENCE: Except Robin.

JEAN: Yes.

LAURENCE: Do you want to call him?

JEAN: I can't. He's fishing with a friend in Michigan.

MARY JO: Call the State Police.

JEAN: No, M.J. It wouldn't matter.

LAURENCE: There's not the slightest chance he'll change his mind, is there?

JEAN: He's not ready, yet, no.

LAURENCE: We can get the wheels in motion around here if you want Robin to come home with you. But understand this:

Miserecordia is a fine place. You needn't worry about the kind
of care he'll get there. You can see him as often as you like.
Why not save yourself some time in hell? Let him go.

JEAN: I can't do that.

LAURENCE: He can't live here forever. And do understand,
Jean, you'll never win this one. I know you think you will, but
you only win this one somewhere in the back of your head, in
some little corner where everybody is Mother Theresa. There is
nothing in the real world to support your fantasy. Let him go to
Miserecordia. Ten tons will come right up off your shoulders if
you do.

JEAN: No.

LAURENCE: Do it.

JEAN *[Rabid]*: I'm telling you, no! He's family, now.

LAURENCE: Then Henry will be packing his bags, I assume?

JEAN: I will keep them both. I don't know how, but I will. I
will "connive" until Robin shows his true colors, or until Henry
does. *[Beat]* I have not misjudged Hal. I have not.
          [The baby blows a raspberry. After a moment:]
I think he just gave me the Bronx cheer. What's the matter,
gummy? What is it?

MARY JO: Looks like he's taking a dump.

LAURENCE: It's the tone of this conversation.

JEAN: He is.

MARY JO: It's a record breaker. Go, baby, go.
          [They laugh at the expression on his face.]
Such relief! Have you ever seen such relief?

LAURENCE: Audrey Hepburn in <u>Charade</u>.

MARY JO: Audrey -- what?

LAURENCE: When she finds the stamps, remember? She gives these priceless stamps to the little kid, thinking they're nothing, and the little kid goes to a dealer, and -

MARY JO: The kid goes to some drug guy? Some junkie?

LAURENCE *[Pearls before swine]:* Yes. Some junkie, Mary Jo. Exactly. Some drug guy. It's tragic.

[Mary Jo is slightly offended, but doesn't know why.]

JEAN: That's better, isn't it? Diaper time?
                         [She offers the bottle to him.]
Are you done with this bottle? Do you want any more of -?
Oh, my God.

MARY JO: Dimples!

[Mary Jo does some sort of Happy Feet Dance. Jean throws her head back and crows. Laurence, who is kneeling next to the chair, grabs Jean by the knees, and shouts encouragement. They have never before, not one of them, seen him smile. Black-out.]

SCENE 3

[The woods. The clearing night sky reveals various constellations in full bloom. Sam has managed a puny little fire. Both he and Henry unpack their gear and attempt to settle into sleeping bags.]

SAM: That's funny. With me, it was always a catcher's mitt.

HENRY: No, pink ballet slippers.

SAM: What else?

HENRY: Pony rides. Trips to the orthodontist. Father-daughter banquets. Sizing up her boyfriends, making them feel just a little uncomfortable. But, eventually, walking her down the aisle.

SAM: Basically, it boils down to Jean. You check out okay?

HENRY: Yeah.

SAM: That means you don't even have to go through this adoption bullshit. If she wants to bring this retarded kid home, fine. It's her choice. But, you tell her what it means.

HENRY: I have too much invested.

SAM: Money well-spent. It taught you a lesson. Life is short. Apply the brakes. Put your foot down.

HENRY: My foot is down. My foot has been down. It's made a hole in the floor boards. My heel is throwing up sparks from the pavement. She hasn't noticed. Besides, I'm not talking about money. I'm talking about Jean.

SAM: Hell, I invested seventeen years, and look what it got me.

HENRY: Sam, it's over between you and Franny because you decided it was over.

SAM *[Flaming]:* I didn't go sneaking around with somebody else. I didn't call the lawyer. I didn't flee to fucking Chicago.

HENRY: And during that time when things were falling apart, did you feel there was nothing you could do to fix them up again?

SAM: No.

HENRY: Was there no event in which you had control? Did she ever want to try again? Did she ever say she'd stop seeing him if you wanted it?

> *[Sam is quiet. Henry is curious.]*

What did you do? What did you say?

SAM: I won't live with a cheat.

HENRY: We're talking about a woman who was faithful for seventeen years, Sam, we are not talking about some floozy. You won't live with a cheat? Is that what you said? She took strong measures, yes. But, then I ask myself, why did she need to employ them?

SAM: I was a good husband, Hal! Come on, for Chrissake! <u>She</u> left me.

HENRY: You were not powerless. You made choices, even if all you decided was to stay quiet or to do nothing. You didn't really think that invective was going to lure her back home, did you? You got what you wanted.

SAM: And what would that be?

HENRY: Escape from the city, the freedom to come back to the woods, to open your own business and start over -- along with the added bonus of sympathy from the neighbor ladies, and drinks from all your pals.

SAM: What a twisted view of adultery. You ought to be a divorce lawyer.

HENRY: Just don't tell me you had no say in the matter. Because I know you did! I know <u>I</u> do. We never achieve what we think we want. We get exactly what we ask for, even when we suppose life is handing us a raw deal. We create every single --

> *[Henry stops, and shakes his head]*

97

What the fuck am I saying?

SAM: It's your feminine side coming out. Just take a deep
breath, think of Chuck Norris, and it will go away.
    [Sam stares at Henry. Henry laughs.]
If what you say is true, what about the bouncing baby boy who
is currently steam-rollering your marriage?

HENRY: You're not serious?

SAM: You brought it up. What is it you were creating when you
brought him into the picture?

HENRY *[Beat]*: You misunderstood me. I only meant to say -

SAM: Goddammit, I did not misunderstand you. I've been
listening very carefully. You said we create our own lives. We
are responsible for what happens to us.

HENRY: For our reaction to what happens to us.

SAM: I got what I wanted when Franny made it with a stranger.
For the moment, I'll choke it down. I'll buy it. It's your turn.
You said your heel is through the floorboards, throwing up
sparks from the pavement. You can't even face a five minute
visit with the little son of a bitch. Why?

HENRY: You're ruthless, you know that, man?

SAM: And you're not? Shit!

HENRY: All right. I'll tell you why. I'll tell you why I can't
face a -- why the hell can't I face a five minute visit with him?
[Silence] Modern medicine is incredible. They can do amazing
things. For instance, five years ago, they told me I had tumors
along my spine and on two of my ribs. This punk-kid surgeon
told me what he and his buddies were gonna do to fix me up.
Two holes front and back, collapse a lung, move the heart to one

side, cut away two vertebrae, and reconstruct the spine with three titanium rods and a few bear claws. He'd yank the two ribs at the last minute, move the heart back, inflate the lung, and staple me back together. The odds were one in twenty I'd bleed to death on the table. If the spinal cord coiled, or if he cut a feeder along the way, then, he said, the odds were one in ten I'd end up paraplegic. Infection during my stay in intensive care was also a hazard. We knew he was the best in his field, so Jean and I listened politely, then hurried right home to examine our other options. There were none. We spent the next few days weeping. I went to a lawyer, and made out a will. She delivered me to the hospital on the appointed day, and we said good-bye without ever using the word. I was trembling on the table as the anesthesiologist began his prep. I comforted myself by thinking about that tunnel they talk about. I was gonna fly through the tunnel, toward the light, and over some little bridge, into a garden where I would throw a little frisbee with all my former pets. They're supposed to be the ones who meet you first, you know: the pets. After a little work-out I'd find the nearest B&B that would take me and five or six dogs. I might nap, get in a shower, and then go out on the town. First, I'd find Nick DeMato and buy him a drink.

SAM: Nick?

HENRY: DeMato, my college room-mate, who was shot by a squirrel the year after we graduated. Then I was gonna mosey over to some cosmic country club and meet my dad for dinner.

SAM: Wait a minute. Back up.

HENRY: That's what I was thinking I'd do.

SAM: Shot by a squirrel?

HENRY: My college room-mate. Shot by a squirrel on a hunting trip near his parents' farm in South Dakota.

SAM: A squirrel shot him? Wait.

HENRY: Through the chest. A bunch of guys, a perfect day in autumn: they were looking for pheasant, so I heard. But it was a slow pheasant day. Nick was bored. He shot a squirrel. The squirrel was lying there in some corn field, looking, for all intents and purposes, cold as a coffin nail. Nick, who was never a trusting soul, approached him, upended his shotgun, and nudged the animal with the butt of it, just to make sure. The little fucker came to life long enough to reach up and put his mitts around the trigger.

SAM: Jesus Christ.

HENRY: I can't wait to ask Nick about it. I'll bet there was a split-second there when he felt like a damned fool.

SAM: I never bet on a sure thing. But, go on. Drinks with Nick?

HENRY: Dinner with my dad. I've missed my Dad. I was thinking he'd be dressed in white linen, with a dry martini in his right hand, and the cigarette that killed him in his left, but . .

SAM: Macabre little evening.

HENRY: But, pleasant enough. Enough to see me through. However, much to my surprise, the hotshot surgeon did just exactly what he said he was going to do. He rebuilt my spine like some mad plumber. I woke up in intensive care, with Jean stroking my forehead. It was all very touch and go; the first few hours were critical. I tried to ask her why they had stuffed a garden hose down my throat. Whoever designed the respirator did not have a grasp on the basic principles of gravity. There are too many heavy tubes, stretched above you, all leading from your mouth to a machine on one side of you. The apparatus that composes your basic respirator is so heavy that it falls to one side, toward the mothership, in a natural attempt to conform itself to the basic laws of gravity. However, unless it is completely centered, one cannot breathe. Understand?

SAM: Yes.

HENRY: And because it is stuffed down one's throat, one cannot talk.

SAM: I see.

HENRY: I was drowning. Also, the nurse in charge of me, her name was Elsie, I will never forget _her_ name - old Elsie kept calling me Harry. "Harry, don't pull at that tube. Harry, lie still." Jean would say, "Elsie, his name is Henry." And, as I coughed up blood, and Jean ran into the hall hollering for Elsie, who disappeared on frequent breaks, old Elsie would meander in and say, "Good sign, Harry, you're expectorating." Well, after the fact, now that's it's been explained to me, I suppose it was a very good sign, but there was no room in Elsie's bedside manner to acknowledge that maybe this wasn't what we were accustomed to in daily life, this coughing of blood -- Oh, fuck.

SAM: Keep going.

HENRY: Elsie was trying to kill me, that was clear. My only hope was Jean. I signaled for paper and pen. Jean dug a pad and pencil out of her purse. I wrote: "I don't trust her." It took every ounce of strength I had to write it down. I remember struggling to lift the pad to her eyes, she looked. I thought I saw a certain degree of shock pass over her face, but she said: "do it again, honey, I can't read it." I wrote the same few words over and over and over. Meanwhile, back at the ranch, Elsie, killer nurse, was scurrying around the bed, shoving that tube deeper into my throat, and more to one side. I wrote to Jean, "Center tube over mouth. Don't let it fall. Can't breathe." Jean struggled to understand, but didn't. I got madder and madder until I was punching myself. She would pull my arms to my side, put the pen into my hand and say: "try it one more time,

101

Hal." I kept thinking, "Jean, listen to the sound of my breath," but she was fixed only on the writing. Finally, when I couldn't lift the pen, I traced words on the bedsheet, and Goddammit, she was watching my hand, but she wasn't listening. Every once in a while she'd say, "I know it's hard." She didn't know squat. This went on from nine o'clock at night until noon the next day. She never left me. But she never got it. She questioned everything Elsie did, but never once mentioned the respirator. The moment they pulled that tube from my throat, and I could breathe and utter sounds again, I let her have it with both barrels. I was so fucking mad at her.

SAM: What did she say?

HENRY: She didn't defend herself. She sat down in a chair. She cried, or laughed, maybe. It was hard to tell. When I saw her do that, I realized --

SAM: What?

HENRY: She knew all the time. She knew if she left me alone, I was going to yank that respirator out.

SAM: So she made you work on penmanship.

HENRY: For fifteen hours.

SAM: Women, Jesus God, they piss me off.

HENRY: *[Beat]* Jean must think that because I court the wheelchair every time I go in for a routine check-up -- she actually must think because I hate the feel of needles, and the smell of alcohol wipes, and the sight of nurses, that I'm afraid of him. Contamination by association, or some damn thing. But, I know what she's up to with that kid, and she's wrong. There is no mad plumber who's gonna rescue him. Jean can stand at that bedside for the rest of his life, and nothing will change.
[Beat]

102

I'm a grown man, and I couldn't <u>abide</u> what they were doing to me. A baby like that should not be made to suffer. I say, Jesus Christ, please, have a little mercy. Don't keep dragging him back. Let him go.

[Beat]

At best he'll lie in a bed for the rest --

SAM: She doesn't care about that.

HENRY: How can she not care if he lies in a bed for the rest of his life!

SAM: She didn't seem to care if you did.

HENRY: I'm her husband! She doesn't even <u>know</u> this boy!

SAM: I don't suppose you remember the night Tom cracked up his motorcycle --

HENRY: Vividly.

SAM: We got to the hospital, and they rushed us to where he was. We sat beside the bed, holding hands, looking down at him. She must have been thinking: hell, whatever the fuck she was thinking, I never knew. But me? I was thinking back to the day I first met him. Franny and I had been going out for about three weeks before she introduced me to him. It was Easter Sunday. We'd gone to church, all three of us, and I was going to spring for a great big breakfast. She said he liked waffles. We were walking toward the front door of Uncle John's Pancake House, holding hands, when the little shit, all of seven-years old, suddenly raced between us, in a terrible rage, screaming, "I break your love." With that, he smashed his arm across our fingers, broke our hands apart, and burst into tears. Franny stooped to talk to him, and I thought to myself, "If I can win this jealous little bugger, I can win her." So that's what I decided to do. I bought him presents. I took him to amusement parks, and circuses. We went fishing, we went to basketball games. I'm the one who brought him home the Harley. All the bribes, all those years, were nothing but an open plea to him to just let me stay close to his mother. Until the night of the accident, I never realized, it was the little bugger who really had the hammerlock on me. The night of the accident, I would have done anything, anything, to keep him alive. Scotch-tape him back together, I don't care. You know, I didn't have a thing to do with bringing that kid into this world, but, I was the only father he was ever going to know, and he was sure as hell my only son. I'd be goddamned if I was going to let him go without a fight. From that Easter morning on, he was my little boy. At the time I married her, everybody thought she was so lucky. I was this white knight, who'd made an honest woman of her at last, who had taken on the support of this snot-nosed kid; but that night in the hospital, looking down at him, I realized for the first time what I must have known all along: I was the lucky one.

[Silence]

HENRY: I see.

SAM: Is she living with this guy yet?

HENRY: No.

SAM: Any plans to?

HENRY: Not that I know of.

SAM *[A beat]*: I never would have left her, no matter how ...

HENRY: No.

SAM: The status quo was bearable, sometimes comfortable.

HENRY: Women don't like things comfortable. They pretend they want it cozy, with their quilts and their throw pillows, but just as you settle in for a nap, they're in your fuckin' face, have you ever noticed that?

104

SAM: Hell, yes. The phone rings: somebody's in crisis, they
gotta go. Or maybe -- maybe they don't like the way you
looked at 'em when you got up that morning, so they gotta sit up
all night and <u>talk</u>. Or company's coming, so they gotta <u>clean</u>.
Not only do <u>they</u> have to clean, but if you want any peace at all,
<u>you</u> have to clean.

HENRY: Yup. Yup.

SAM: Well, shit.

HENRY: Take this. Cut me off. *[He tosses the bottle of vodka
to Sam.]*

SAM: Shit, man.

HENRY: Knock yourself out.

SAM: Did you bring aspirin, by any chance?

HENRY: The knapsack at your feet.

*[Sam goes for the small bottle, opens it, swallows two, and
swigs. He replaces the bottle and then settles back. Henry looks
out at the clearing sky.]*

> "I am content to follow to its source
> Every event in action or in thought;
> Measure the lot; forgive myself the lot!
> When such as I cast out remorse
> So great a sweetness flows into the breast
> We must laugh and we must sing,
> We are blessed by everything,
> Every thing we look upon is blest."

SAM *[Pause]*: Keats?

HENRY: Yeats, Sam.

SAM: Okay, so. Yeats.

[Black out.]

ACT V

SCENE 1

[The hospital. Rademacher, Laurence and Mary Jo stand a certain distance from the crib.]

RADEMACHER: Have you tried to reach her?

LAURENCE: I called her father's place. The line's been disconnected.

RADEMACHER: Are you sure? That's impossible. Are you certain?

LAURENCE: Show me the number you've got.
                    [Rademacher does.]
Six-seven-two-two. That's the number I've been calling. It's no longer in service.

RADEMACHER: Well, now what? What are we going to do? What do you suggest?

MARY JO: Have you tried Jean?

LAURENCE: Since nine o'clock. Nobody's there.

MARY JO: She's on her way, then.

RADEMACHER: Mrs. Farrell cannot sign the releases.

LAURENCE *[Irritated]*: We know that, Viv. We'll keep trying Emma Miller, okay?

RADEMACHER: What about the mother?

LAURENCE: Which mother?

RADEMACHER: Emma's mother. The mother of the mother.

LAURENCE: She is listed on my chart as deceased.

RADEMACHER: According to the DCFS report, she's very much alive. She has an address and telephone number.

LAURENCE: That's not what I've got.

RADEMACHER: I have a phone number here. Let's try it. Try it!

LAURENCE: Would you get out of my face with the paper, Viv? I've had a rotten night. Enough already. Yes, give it to me.

RADEMACHER *[Showing him]*: Right there.

[Jean, freshly scrubbed, walks in.]

JEAN: Good morning.

LAURENCE *[Replacing the phone in its cradle]*: Hello.

MARY JO: Hello, Jean.

RADEMACHER: Mrs. Farrell.

JEAN: Here's clean laundry. *[She drops a plastic bag at her feet. She holds a brown paper parcel in her arms.]* And, don't tell the adults on the floor, because we don't want any carnage, a genuine Barney doll. What a coup!

LAURENCE: I tried to call you.

JEAN *[He has never called before]*:   You did? What for?

LAURENCE: Come here. Come sit with me.

JEAN: No.

LAURENCE: Come on, Jean, sit with me for a minute.

JEAN: Where is he?

LAURENCE: He's in his crib.

JEAN: What's he doing?

LAURENCE: Let me tell you what happened.
                    [Laurence extends his hands to her.]

JEAN *[The beginning of a wail]*:   Wait a minute. Wait. Wait.

[Cross-fade]

SCENE 2

[The offices of Family Resources. A young pregnant woman waits by herself. She looks at the posters on the walls, paces. Tess McGarrett enters.]

TESS: Michelle? How are you doing?

MICHELLE: I wouldn't mind stepping out for a smoke.

TESS: They're here. They're in Alan's office. It'll be just another minute or two. Can you wait?

MICHELLE: Sure.

TESS: Are you nervous?

MICHELLE: I'm just wondering what I'm doing here.

TESS: Michelle, if you have any doubts, won't you please tell me now? You are, of course, free to change your mind any time up to three days after the birth, but I have to tell you, if you're not sure, you'd be doing this couple a big favor by saying so now.

MICHELLE: I won't change my mind. I just want to meet them and get on with it.
                    [There is a gentle knock.]

TESS: Now's your chance.
                    [She opens the door.]
    Hi. Come on in.

                    [Henry and Jean enter.]

MICHELLE: Hi.

HENRY: Hello.

TESS: This is Michelle. Michelle, this is Henry and Jean.

HENRY: It's nice meeting you.

MICHELLE: You, too.

JEAN *[Tight]*: Hello.

MICHELLE *[There is an awkward silence, and then Michelle laughs]*: I've been reading about you.

HENRY: You saw the album?

MICHELLE: I liked the family reunion, and 10th Annual

Softball Game.

TESS: Why don't we sit down?

MICHELLE: Okay.

HENRY *[After a moment]*: How are you feeling?

MICHELLE: Big as a barn, and my feet hurt all the time, but they say she's in good shape.

HENRY: It's a little girl?

MICHELLE: Oh, yeah, didn't they tell you?

HENRY: No.

MICHELLE: Due December 9th.

HENRY: That's soon.

MICHELLE: Yes. Pretty soon.

TESS: I can't help but notice the resemblance between you and Jean, Michelle.

MICHELLE: You look like my Aunt Carol. She was an ice skater.

JEAN: Oh. Thank you.

MICHELLE: I also liked the idea that you were from different religious backgrounds. *[To Henry:]* And you're in the arts?

HENRY: Yes.

MICHELLE: I always wanted to be a dancer. *[To Henry:]* I know you're a writer, but I don't guess I've ever read anything

110

you've written.

HENRY: You're among the vast majority, then. Don't feel bad.

MICHELLE: I have lots of questions to ask you. I hope you don't mind.

JEAN *[Reserved]*: No. That's good. I have some questions, too.

MICHELLE: Should I just start?

TESS: Why not?

MICHELLE: Okay. These are stupid, some of them, but just to get the conversation going -- *[She clears her throat.]* Henry, how do you feel your life has prepared you for fatherhood?

HENRY: That's not at all a stupid question. Huh. I've lived my life very selfishly. It was just about what was best for <u>me</u>, what I needed and wanted for myself. My career was important. It wasn't until I met Jean that I began to feel it was time to consider other things. I think, when we tried to have a baby of our own -- I don't know if they told you --

MICHELLE: A little. I know you tried for a long time.

HENRY: When it didn't work the way we assumed it would, deprivation was our greatest teacher.

MICHELLE: Deprivation?

HENRY: We'd lost out on something precious, that most people take for granted. More than anything, that sense of loss has prepared me for fatherhood. I wouldn't have been a good father if it had happened when I was twenty, or even thirty. It's been a long, wanting time, during which I've had to think, and to decide exactly what kind of father I want to be.

MICHELLE: Do you have anything to add, Jean?

JEAN *[Politely]*: No.

MICHELLE: Okay. My next question is for Jean: if things work out between us, what do you think you can offer to this child?

JEAN: What can I offer?

MICHELLE: As a mother, what can you offer?

JEAN: What can I offer?

MICHELLE: Yes.

JEAN: Myself. All my love.

MICHELLE: What are the little, day to day things?

JEAN: Time. Effort. My hands. My voice. My lap. We like to go places. We have a wonderful home. We love books and the beach. Music. We like music. All kinds of it. *[Warming to her subject.]* I have a music box. My Grandparents gave it to me years ago.
                    [Cross-fade begins]
I've been saving it. I want my own child to have it.

MICHELLE: This may sound awful, but -- ever since I got pregnant, I feel like I've been baby-sitting. Watching over this child for somebody else. She isn't mine.

                    [Cross-fade]

LAURENCE: Can I call Henry for you?

MICHELLE: I've taken care of her for somebody else.

112

SCENE 3

[The Hospital]

LAURENCE: Where's Henry? Is Henry near a phone?

JEAN: Not until Tuesday.

LAURENCE: What about your friend, Mrs. Stornant?

JEAN: She went back to New York. Yesterday. How's that for impeccable timing?

LAURENCE: I'll get someone to drive you home.

JEAN: Why is the side of his face purple?

LAURENCE: The blood has stopped flowing, you understand? It stops, and settles.

JEAN: It's a hell of a time to ask, but was he baptized?

LAURENCE: Emma had him baptized the first time she came up, but, you're not gonna like it: he's a Methodist, kiddo.

JEAN *[Laughs, in spite of herself]*: No, that's fine. He's so little. So little.

LAURENCE: I've looked after babies like Robin in the past. They're usually irritable. You can understand it, because of the pressure on the skull and the spine. But, he never complained.

MARY JO: He was champ material.

JEAN: And, yesterday!

MARY JO: I know!

LAURENCE: That was incredible!

JEAN: It was probably gas.

LAURENCE *[With the slightest edge]*: Nothing of the kind.

JEAN: What happens, now?

LAURENCE: Rademacher just talked to Emma's mother, and there's an all out search. Her mother never knew about Robin, never even knew she was pregnant.

JEAN: I'm not surprised.

LAURENCE: Emma will tell us what she wants done with him.

JEAN: I was pushing him. I should have told him to take it in gradual stages.

LAURENCE: So, you were a nudge. Every good mother is a bit of a nudge. You never really bought the party line. This kid was going to get better, and that's all there was to it. So, he did! I think he hung on just to see what crazy massage technique you were gonna bring in next. He was getting stronger. He was taking food on his own. He was figuring out his own little shunt system.

JEAN: If he was doing all that -- then why?

MARY JO: Maybe he didn't want to cause trouble at home.

JEAN: What?

LAURENCE: We knew from the beginning, Jean.

JEAN: Did you try to resuscitate?

LAURENCE: Emma left instructions not to.

JEAN *[A lifelong regret is born]*: Oh. Of course.
                         [Beat]
Where's Emma? We wait for Emma?

LAURENCE: There are a few things we can do in the mean time.

JEAN: What?

LAURENCE: Why don't we get him dressed? What do you think he would like to be wearing?

JEAN: The Cubs uniform.

MARY JO: Cubs, definitely.

LAURENCE: We all agree for once. With the argyles?

JEAN: Are they clean?

LAURENCE: Got 'em right here. Would you like to do it?

JEAN: You do the uniform, and I'll do the socks.

LAURENCE: Good thinking.
                    [They dress the child.]

MARY JO: What about his possessions? Would you like them?

JEAN: No, leave the doll. Is it clean?

MARY JO: He only spit up on it a hundred and sixty-two times, but miraculously, today it's clean.

JEAN: Humpty was his whipping boy, I'm afraid. Let's put in the A&D ointment, too, just in case. And the Walkman. He'll need the tapes, of course.

115

MARY JO: And the music box?

JEAN: He never had shoes, did he?

MARY JO: The music box, Jean?

JEAN: I should have brought him some sneakers. Black high
 tops.
> *[Mary Jo tucks the music box beside him.]*

LAURENCE: Do you want to say anything?

JEAN: Say anything?

LAURENCE: To him. Some final words.

JEAN *[simply]*: I will blow kisses heavenward; shooting stars that
 will fall on your tummy, and your cheeks, and the soles of your
 feet. When you least expect them, they will rain down on you,
 and they will warm you, when you need warming, and they will
 make you laugh, when you feel alone, and they will remind you,
 when you need to remember. I will always love you, and I will
 always remember.

LAURENCE *[Waiting, and then:]*: You want to say anything,
 Mary Jo?

MARY JO *[Honored]*: Oh, yes.

LAURENCE: By all means.

MARY JO: I just wanna say that he was an awesome kid, and
 I'm sorry Jean never got a chance to spring him. <u>Go</u>, Bud! Find
 the beat, Babe!

LAURENCE *[Piously waiting for more, he suddenly realizes she's
 done]*: Is that it?

MARY JO: Go. Talk.

LAURENCE: Thank you, Mary Jo. How eloquent. *[Dismissing her, he looks down at Robin's face:]* Dear Heavenly Father, take Jean's child, Robin, in Your Arms. He has had a tremendous journey, however brief. He stands before you, a spiffy little character, in a baseball jacket and argyle socks. Please note: the dreaded tube is gone, no mean achievement. He is a child of valor and of heart. There is a trinity here on earth that stretches loving arms to You in the fervent hope that You will nourish and encourage this brave boy forever. Bring comfort to his grieving mother. May we four meet again in joyful reunion. Eternal rest grant unto him, O Lord. And let perpetual light shine upon him. May he rest in peace. Amen.

MARY JO: Amen.

LAURENCE: Stay as long as you like.

[Laurence and Mary Jo leave silently. Jean looks down at Robin for a while. She picks up the music box, winds it, and listens for less than three seconds. She snaps it shut, and like some guilty thief, puts it in her purse. She returns to his side. Henry appears in the door, dressed as he was on the fishing trip. He is equipped with teddy bear and balloon. He stands rather awkwardly with a smile on his face. She turns, sees him. He walks toward her. Black out.]

THE BABY

Robin Andrew Miller

Naturally, Robin is a problem for the properties department.
What follows is a rather technical description of the child. He
would have weighed a little over eleven pounds at birth. He
should weigh approximately thirteen pounds as the play opens.
His body is fourteen inches long, from his toes to his shoulders,
and this expanse contains a little under half of his total body
weight. From his shoulders to the top of his head, he measures
approximately fourteen inches. The circumference of his head
measures approximately twenty-two inches. It is bulbous, and,
from the browline to the crown, full of water. It is crucial that
moving with this baby in one's arms is an off-center, slightly
terrifying experience. He is always cloaked from audience view
by the isolette, or by blankets. The absolute realism that would
require George Lucas' hand is to be avoided, as is the other
extreme: pantomime.